Praise

'In *HumanForce: The power of emotions in a changing workplace*, author, entrepreneur and coach, Natalie Boudou, speaks truth to the reality that almost everything we do relates to emotions. This insightful and practical book is backed by decades of working with leaders and organisations, top scientific research on emotions and her personal experiences of co-raising her autistic child. Boudou's insights are what leaders need to harness the power of emotions – both energy depleting and energy uplifting – to dramatically impact performance and happiness, both for themselves and those who they lead.'
— Amanda Shantz, Professor of Management and MBA Director, University of St. Gallen

'Natalie delves into the essence of what makes a workplace human; how we navigate the waves of emotions at work, with our teams and in our daily lives. She reveals one of the best kept secrets of successful leaders: by using the power of emotions and reading through the multiple signals that they send, we can make better decisions and enable better working environments for people. We can have it all: happiness, balance, wellbeing and performance at work. Thank you Natalie for sharing and revealing the secret'
— Elise Buckle, CEO of Climate and Sustainability, Co-Founder of SHE Changes Climate – UN Advisor and International Gender Champion

'How do you ensure that your team members remain motivated, efficient, happy, inspired over the long term? Through an out-of-the box analysis of different soft skills, enriched with practical examples. In *HumanForce*, Natalie Boudou gives us the key to an innovating and inspiring leadership.'
— Anne Sophie Eyméoud, Director General
Rothschild & Co Wealth Management, Belgium

'As Natalie has reinforced so eloquently that leading with empathy and emotion and personal vulnerability is an absolute must to connect, inspire and build a culture of belonging. I have done this throughout my career, and it really works.'
— Mike Piker, Global DE&I and Reward Director,
Flutter Entertainment

'The Great Resignation, quiet quitting and employee burnout are terms used frequently in the headlines of articles trying to decipher the reality of the modern workplace for employers and their battle to retain talent against a tide of disengaged employees. Natalie Boudou explores the reality behind the headlines, tackling the complex subject of emotions in the workplace which, if acknowledged and managed well, make all the difference for employee well-being, sense of belonging and connection. Her book, *HumanForce: The power of emotions in a changing workplace* should be read by employers aiming to learn how to harness emotions to enable employees to be their authentic selves. Employees themselves will also benefit from the insights in the book to increase their awareness of how to navigate bringing their authentic self to the workplace. In the battle for talent, more focus on emotions could make all

the difference to gain and retain employees who want and need to work for an employer that cares. As Natalie demonstrates throughout the book, this is at the heart of strong company performance.'
— Charlotte Lindsey Curtet, Chief Public Policy Officer, CyberPeace

'*HumanForce* places emotions at the centre of our working lives. In this fluent and clearly written book, we can all learn how to become more aware of our own complex emotions, before we regulate and apply them in our professional lives and in the workplace. Drawing on the most recent research and using clear examples, *HumanForce* is essential reading because it provides us all with a blueprint on how to create more harmonious workplaces and professional relationships.'
— Maleiha Malik, Professor of Law, Kings College London

'In this digital age, human emotional connection is increasingly at odds with the Internet. However, while helping humans overcome communication difficulties, automation technology is also proving the importance and irreplaceability of human's most traditional emotional communication. *HumanForce* has made me realise that the ideal social organisation should not only be efficient, but also have warmth.'
— Xiangchen Zhang, Deputy Director-General, WTO and Ambassador

'As we enter into the post-COVID era, the role of emotions can no longer be minimized or ignored. Employees, managers and everyone in the work force are solidly refusing to participate in their careers any longer

as cogs in a machine. People understand that their time, their goals, and their purpose are all intertwined in how they spend their careers, so the tide has turned from running a work force to nurturing a human force. *Human Force: The power of emotions in a changing workplace* is a thought-provoking piece that considers these issues from both a high-level vantage point, and from a ground-level managerial perspective. Offering both broad perspectives and tangible models, Natalie Boudou guides readers through a realistic vision of how human potential can be optimized for the mutual benefit of employers and employees. This book offers practical perspective for HR professionals, MBA students, managers, and anyone seeking to make an impact through their career.'
— Dr Rebecca Nicholson, Ph.D., Author of *Executive Sexism and Natural Healing as Conflict Resolution*

'Natalie's analysis and thought leadership around how we bring our emotions to work and what that means for our careers and workplace culture is absolutely brilliant.

'We need a more understanding and empathetic workplace and Natalie's work is a major contribution to helping us get there.

'I think this book is essential reading for all leaders and managers. The more we can understand ourselves, and the wider context around emotions, bias and culture, the better off we will all be.'
— Elliott Rae, Speaker, Author, Founder and Editor-in-Chief, Music.Football.Fatherhood

'This is a wonderful journey through the world of emotions and provides practical tools to help address the challenges life throws at us. Grounded in centuries of thinking and presented in a language we can all relate to ... a great read!'
— John McCusker, Global Vice-President of Talent Management, Bacardi

Human F●rce

THE POWER OF EMOTIONS IN A CHANGING WORKPLACE

NATALIE BOUDOU

R^ethink

First published in Great Britain in 2023
by Rethink Press (www.rethinkpress.com)

© Copyright Natalie Boudou

To my husband, Fabrice, one of the most emotionally intelligent men I know, to my son Max who is following in his father's footsteps and to my daughter Elise whose journey is a great example of the Human Force

Contents

Introduction

Almost everything we do relates to emotions. Yet, despite the fact we all experience a range of emotions all the time, there is still a widespread reluctance to talk about them; or, at least, the ones we find painful. If we do talk about them at all, we do so in the context of categorising emotions as 'positive' or 'negative'.

While we are mostly relaxed about expressing what we consider as pleasant emotions, such as happiness, passion or engagement, the shutters go up for anything that doesn't feel good to us. This way of being is enshrined in our language, with an entire catalogue of expressions dedicated to vilifying unwanted emotions such as sadness, embarrassment or shame – and shutting down any further discussion about them.

'Pull yourself together,' one person will admonish another, in an apparent bid to help them move on.

'Sort yourself out.'

'Get a grip.'

Read any literary or philosophy work throughout history and emotions (even so-called 'positive' emotions) are rarely portrayed in a positive light. They get in the way or interfere with the choices we should make. Judgement and rational thought are the qualities we should respect, or so the thinking goes. It's better that things come from the head rather than the heart.

The common theme is clear: baring our emotions is a weakness. For added spin, derogatory labels such as 'histrionic' or 'hysterical' imply there is a terrible tipping point between giving in to this 'weakness' and a complete loss of control. These insulting terms are mostly directed at women, although occasionally they're used to belittle men too in a seeming attempt to isolate those who exhibit a healthy connection with their feelings.

I started questioning these catch-all labels at an early age. My family, in particular my mother, would often tell me that I was too emotional or 'highly strung'. My young brain went from contemplating whether I did, indeed, have more emotions than anybody else to wondering if it was really such a bad thing to be too emotional. The use of the adverb 'too' certainly implied as much. I was *excessively* emotional.

This sparked a lifelong interest in emotions and led to a career specialising in the subject. In particular, I was drawn to how emotions are viewed in the workplace. While the odd meltdown is apparently permitted within the safety of our own homes, emotions are frowned upon in many corporate settings.

For some reason, all our emotions are expected to evaporate somewhere along the way on our commute to work.

The truth is, there is no such thing as being *too* emotional, whether it is at home or at work. Likewise, there aren't positive emotions and negative emotions. The definition of positive and negative emotions is a supposedly neat polarisation between those that feel good in the moment and those that feel bad in the moment, but for me that distinction is not ideal. Indeed, emotions which feel positive in the moment may not actually be helpful in the long term and vice versa.

As for those emotions that are difficult and unpleasant in the moment, rather than label them as negative, I prefer to call them *energy draining* because that's exactly what they do. They drain our energy.

You may recognise the scenario: you are at home and in a bad way. Perhaps work hasn't gone well or you've suffered some sort of personal crisis. By the end of the day, you feel exhausted, almost as if you've just run a marathon. You're absolutely washed-out, even though you haven't made any physical effort whatsoever. You are experiencing energy-draining emotions.

Energy draining or otherwise, every emotion is simply a message and there to serve a purpose. Emotions have something to tell us. If we humans didn't have emotions, our species wouldn't have survived for so long. They have helped us grow and evolve.

We need to embrace *all* our emotions because they play a crucial role in every aspect of our lives. They:

- Protect us

- Are key to how we think and react

- Help us motivate ourselves and make decisions

- Help us not only understand ourselves, but also understand and connect with others

Without a doubt, emotions are the fundamental building blocks of our lives.

We are not at the mercy of our emotions. Showing emotions is not a weakness or a sign of loss of control. Quite the opposite, in fact. Instead of showing a stiff upper lip (there's another one of those vilifying expressions), what we should be doing is learning how to identify emotions, process how we feel, and then work with those emotions effectively. Apply this strategy and we can achieve so much more – and feel much better about ourselves.

Sure, you could carry on ignoring your emotions at work (subtext: 'Everyone else does, so I don't want to stand out'), but ignoring an emotion doesn't mean it simply disappears. Consider them on a par with that work-day staple, the ubiquitous email. Emotions are like messages in your inbox. It's up to you whether you click on the message to see what it has to say.

You could ignore it, letting it pile up with dozens of other unopened and ignored emotional missives, but like its digital counterpart, an emotion won't just disappear unless you take some sort of action. You can't simply forget it. That ignored emotional prompt will come back and find you. It will be there when you can't fall asleep at night, or when you have a headache, or when you feel down the next day. There will be reminder after reminder until you *can't help* but pay attention.

Anyone who has ever made the decision to purge a bulging inbox of hundreds or even thousands of emails and succeeded in the endeavour will truly understand the pleasure of feeling like they've finally got their life under control. It is the same with emotions. Deal with them, harness the power and work with them.

I've been working in the corporate setting for some years now, helping team leaders and individuals on their teams to work more effectively with their emotions. The goal is to build stronger, more intelligent workplaces through cultural transformation. This is not a one-size-fits-all process. At the risk of stating the obvious, all teams are made up of individuals, yet it is not uncommon for business leaders to search for a single answer to motivate what they call their workforce.

This is entirely wrong. Workforce implies the team is a homogenous group with no discernibly different characteristics. Are you exactly the same as your colleagues? Of course not. At work, as at home, we are individual, unique human beings, each with something quite different to give.

It would be far more appropriate to call our teams a humanforce because that is entirely what they are. They are the life and heartbeat of any workplace.

Over the years, I have seen many examples of what happens when a team is dismissed as the 'workforce' and the emotional needs of individuals are ignored. I've worked with clients who are burned out or well on the way to being so thanks to chronic stress. There have been countless individuals who have told me they are on the brink of resigning because they can no longer work with toxic leaders who have zero emotional awareness about the challenges they are facing. I've seen people who have lost their sense of self-worth and belonging. In every case, the result of this poor emotional intelligence or emotional quotient (EQ) in the workplace has been a poorly performing, highly dysfunctional environment.

Equally, I have seen many examples of the power of emotions when they are understood and leveraged properly. When business leaders understand their own emotional responses and are sensitive to the emotions in others, it can transform a workplace, building a strong, happy humanforce.

Once you 'get' why humanforce is so much more powerful than workforce, there is no going back. It is the key to better, stronger, more emotionally intelligent workplaces. Through my consultancy of the same name, I work with organisations and help their leaders understand how they can better engage their own humanforce by recognising everyone for the individuals they are and creating an environment where employees believe they can bring their whole unique selves to work.

Whether we are focusing on health and well-being, diversity and inclusion, or building strong leadership, EQ is one of the foundations for success. We are all driven by a need to belong and to be recognised for our contribution. It is not an impossible challenge for businesses. There just needs to be a will to change.

What to expect from this book

During the COVID-19 pandemic I, like many people, took the opportunity for some quiet reflection. I decided to document what I had learned about working with emotions and the potential of a human-force. When I started to write this book, we were still in lockdown. The working world had changed immeasurably with many teams scattered far and wide, grappling with the challenges of home working and all sorts of new technology.

However, it was a time when there were faint glimmers of hope that we'd come out of the pandemic before too long, so we began to imagine what life would look like when it was all over. Of course, we all hoped for a much better future once we'd fully emerged from such an extraordinary experience.

We all now know this has not happened. It is clear to nearly everyone that while the workplace has fundamentally changed, it has not necessarily been for the better. While many firms have (in some cases reluctantly) embraced hybrid working and, indeed, some had begun this process even before the pandemic, the results have been variable.

It is rare to come across business leaders who have perfected the art of connecting their geographically distant teams on an emotional level. Few have yet worked out how to create a sense of belonging among employees who rarely set foot in their offices or see colleagues face to face. A large number of business leaders I work with have confided that they see a huge uphill battle ahead to reconnect and reunite their teams. There is also a significant job to be done to recover from the emotional fallout of the COVID-19 period and build new resilience going forward.

My goal for this book is to help this recovery process through my experience of and knowledge about working with emotions. I have documented how leaders and teams can work more effectively together to build a new understanding among themselves and begin creating a workplace fit for the twenty-first century.

There are plenty of tips and strategies here, which have been learned through many years spent coaching and supporting leaders and their teams on how to work more effectively with their emotions and the emotions of others, but making an impact will involve more than simply implementing these tools. There needs to be a strategic approach to creating a culture of belonging. To explain how this works, I have documented my own previous experiences, both good and bad, of working as a professional in the private and not-for-profit sector to make suggestions on how to build a more emotionally intelligent workplace.

You can use and apply many of the strategies in your private life too. My own personal journey supporting my autistic daughter Elise played a significant role in my interest in emotions and my decision to write this book. Anxiety was a staple part of my life while Elise was growing up. As my husband and I navigated all the fears and uncertainties that came with raising a child with special needs, EQ played a huge role in our parenting.

In my own case, I found it essential to be able to recognise my anxiety, becoming more aware of my emotions and their impact on others. My resilience grew alongside my emotional agility. Over time, I became more at ease with and adept at making necessary adjustments and being flexible when necessary.

Communication between ourselves and with our family, as well as the supportive relationships that we both cultivated around us, was key to the wellbeing of myself and my husband. We actively looked for joyful moments to celebrate progress and recognised the achievements of our child whenever we could. It was all crucial in getting us to where we are today. All of this, of course, flowed into my coaching and training.

This book makes use of the latest academic research into emotions and you will find that I have shared many studies which I found hugely helpful in my own research. If you are the type of person who enjoys 'the science part', I would urge you to consult the references and read further. There are some fascinating insights there.

I have also spoken with a wide range of emotional and behavioural experts, as well as senior executives from public and private organisations, and included a number of their contributions. Their views on the role of emotions in the workplace have helped shape my thoughts for this book and offer a broad viewpoint, thanks to their wide range of backgrounds.

We are standing on the threshold of a once-in-a-lifetime opportunity to change our workplaces for the better. If you give it some thought, you may find yourself feeling nervous or apprehensive, excited or optimistic. That's all fine; it means you are already tuning in to how you feel.

As you will discover, there is no such thing as a 'bad' emotion. What you need to do next is to learn to work with your emotions so you can take active steps to make the changes we all need to see.

Let's unleash the power of the humanforce together.

PART ONE
WHAT ARE EMOTIONS AND WHY ARE THEY SO IMPORTANT?

ONE

Why Emotions Count At Work

It's been dubbed the Great Resignation. Around the world, post-pandemic, record numbers were quitting their jobs. Stories abounded about how COVID-19 made us rethink our lives and finally pursue our dream career. Mid-level employees retrained as teachers, shop workers started online stores selling handicrafts, and top executives swapped the boardroom for small home-based operations.

Meanwhile, major organisations from McDonald's to Amazon were scrambling to fill the open positions left behind, offering triple- or even quadruple-figure hiring bonuses. Yet, while it is indeed true that millions were searching for meaningful long-term change, this trend had been steadily growing for more than a decade before the pandemic, when the monthly average rate of people quitting their jobs had risen by 0.1 percentage points a year.[1]

What was going on?

At least part of the shift was down to pure demographics as vast numbers of Baby Boomers left the workplace for good. It was not so much the Great Resignation as the Great Retirement, but that doesn't tell the whole story. Far from it.

What we were and, at the time of writing, are still seeing is a shift in perspective. Employees of all ages are reconsidering the role of work in their lives for a range of reasons. Ranking high are low pay, lack of opportunities and feeling disrespected at work.[2] There's a real sense that we want something more from the workplace. Millennials and Generation Z in particular want a workplace culture that is supportive, inclusive, transparent and trustworthy. These cohorts, which make up nearly half of the workforce, look towards their place of employment for a sense of purpose and want to feel in control and empowered.[3] Most of all, they want an *emotional* connection.

The cost of ignoring emotions in the workplace

I've been watching the rise and rise of prioritising emotions in the workplace with a high degree of interest. It's been a long time coming. When I started out my career as a lawyer in the early 1990s, the firm which employed me appeared to pride itself on its macho, old-fashioned environment. My colleagues were very guarded and I rarely saw any displays of emotion around me.

As an already keen observer of emotions, I got the definite sense my co-workers felt an obligation to suppress theirs to look professional. It wasn't just my workplace either. In every business I encountered, both leaders and employees alike seemed to have an unspoken agreement that emotions were not useful. In fact, they could be a wholly unwelcome interruption or interference in the day-to-day. Anyone who brought emotions into the workplace would negatively impact productivity and performance.

Since then, things have changed, albeit slowly. It has been generally accepted that emotion affects collaboration and teamwork and that our interactions with colleagues do have an impact on performance. Even so, as the gathering pace of the Great Resignation implies, there is still a long way to go.

While it has become accepted practice to offer employees lengthy inductions on how to schedule meetings, craft emails to the company style and follow health and safety process, there is still little direction from employers on what to do if we are upset with a colleague or feel a meeting with the boss went badly. The onus is on us as individuals to think more deeply about our approach to work. Hardly surprisingly, many of us are not sure how emotional we can be. What is the best way to interact with colleagues? What emotions are OK to show in the workplace? What emotions should we keep in check? *Are we too emotional?*

If the statistics are anything to go by, we could summarise the answers to these questions by saying that displaying 'too much' emotion is still largely frowned upon. Research released just a few months before the pandemic showed that 30% of line managers considered the expression of emotions at work to be a weakness, while 51% believed emotions should be suppressed altogether in a professional context.[4]

Even if this hostility to expressing ourselves is not overtly voiced, the message comes through loud and clear. We instinctively know that we can't bring our true selves to work. A third of workers admit to actively concealing their real emotions by putting on 'a positive face' at work.[5] Nearly double that amount (59%) reported feeling emotions at work they didn't believe they could freely express. When it comes to sadness, 60% chose to manage it themselves rather than asking for help.

Stifling our emotions or not talking about them is very unhealthy and can lead to worrying long-term consequences for our mental health. For clear insight into the fact that the way we work today isn't working, check out these results from a poll of full-time employees in the United States:[6]

- 84% report at least one workplace factor that negatively impacts their mental health

- 76% experienced at least one symptom of a mental-health challenge in the past year

- 50% have left their jobs due, at least in part, to mental-health reasons

- Eight days on average are missed due to mental-health problems

- 72% of capacity is what workers report operating at, when considering mental health

It doesn't help that we are currently facing an epidemic of loneliness, feeling that we have no one to turn to at home or at work. In one survey, 36% admitted feeling lonely 'frequently' or 'almost all of the time',[7] and there are increasing signs of anxiety and depression. Thanks to growing numbers of single-person households, which have become the second most common home arrangement behind couples without young children,[8] many people look to the workplace for human-to-human connection and an uplifting feeling of community. Yet, this need is still largely being ignored.

In many ways, it is astonishing that this situation has been allowed to endure for so long. Aside from the human impact, unhappy, disengaged employees don't make any business sense.

It has long been recognised that high employee engagement leads to better job satisfaction, more sales and improved revenue. Companies with highly engaged teams boast 21% higher productivity than those without.[9] Yet, more than half of employees feel disengaged (51%) and 13% actively so

To be clear: being disengaged at work means feeling miserable and spreading negativity to colleagues. Disengagement leads to lack of motivation and a low sense of responsibility, resulting in poor productivity, errors at work, missed deadlines, poor customer service and missed profits. It also, as the Great Resignation suggests, leads to more job switching.

It's not just that we don't feel fulfilled, though; our workplaces can be bad for our health. We are seeing an unprecedented rise in chronic stress and burnout as employees respond negatively to increased workloads, the always-on culture and unreasonable expectations.

The impact of technology

There is perhaps one highly significant influencing factor in the gulf between what employees want from their careers versus employer expectations. Even before the pandemic, the workplace had been steadily undergoing the biggest shift since the Industrial Revolution.

Technology has transformed the way we work. In almost every sector, we must now deal with a plethora of apps, communications tools and project management software. The vast majority is designed from the employer's point of view, piling on the pressure for everyone on the workforce to be more productive, constantly in touch and fully accountable for every decision.

Thanks to smartphones and high-speed internet, we've slipped into an always-on culture where work is rarely confined to the workplace or standard working hours. We're overloaded with interruptions; the average worker receives 121 emails a day and checks in on them once every six minutes.[10] Our inboxes are stuffed full of requests and urgent matters to deal with. It. Never. Stops.

Meanwhile, not everyone embraces technology (even Millennials and Gen Zs who came of age in the internet age). A lot of us find the endless procession of new tools unnecessarily complex and intimidating. All the while, there is an undercurrent of insecurity that if we can't step up and keep up to date, we can be replaced by someone who can.

It's one of the most recent iterations of technology that is causing the most alarm: artificial intelligence (AI). AI has long been the staple of dystopian movies; from *The Terminator* to *The Matrix* to *Ex Machina*, the machines are regarded with great suspicion. *They're coming for us*, is the common thread.

With AI, everything will change at home, work and play, and not necessarily in a good way. To date, the workplace is where we most often encounter the forward-thinking technological breakthroughs, yet while machine learning and AI have already produced some exciting changes and are a key part of modernisation and efficiency, there's a certain amount of resistance. What does all of this mean for us human beings? How will the machines redefine the added value we bring to the workplace?

The signs are not good. One of the most recent developments in AI is artificial EQ, or emotion AI. This remarkable-sounding tech claims machines can detect human emotions in exactly the same way as you or I. Emotion AI has already been used in the interview process, weighing up candidates versus existing top performers on the team based on micro expressions, tone of voice and other variables. Other programs are being used to judge if we are distracted while we work or about to make a risky move.

Billions of pounds are being poured into emotion AI initiatives to find out more about our thoughts and help make us better workers. What a brave new world.

Right now, there is a lot of discussion about whether it is even possible for AI to properly gauge human emotions (the result of which may or may not pave the way towards certain Armageddon). Emotions are complicated. They develop and change according to our cultures and lived experiences. This one-size-fits-all approach to detection could lead to discrimination. Unfair outcomes will be difficult to challenge, because 'machines don't lie'.

You will no doubt have your own views on this, as have I. Primarily, I believe that there is one thing AI can never do and that is be human. It can't leverage emotions as we can. Even if AI becomes able to recognise and mimic our emotions, it will never be able to achieve the same warmth, empathy and compassion. Skills such as motivating, understanding and interacting with each other will still be done better by humans and these skills are based on EQ. Human emotions will give us the edge when it comes to inspiring employees, creating trust, bonding and belonging.

Emotions at work in a post-pandemic world

All of this had been developing for a while before 2020. Then, along came the pandemic, which exacerbated so many of the issues detailed here. Millions of people were furloughed or lost their jobs, while others had to adapt to working from home. Those workers who did have to continue to work, such as those in hospitals, shops and warehouses, found themselves abruptly facing new practices to help stop transmission of the virus.

Initially, most of us confidently expected to go back to normal within a matter of weeks. There would be a hard date. One day, we'd be working at home or under stringent COVID-19 protocols, and the next we'd be back to our usual work environment like nothing had happened. Yet, despite numerous organisations across multiple sectors setting firm get-back-to-normal dates, plans were repeatedly pushed back as the pandemic dragged on. By year three of COVID-19, most firms had not only stopped trying to predict a constantly moving target, they had also begun to accept it was improbable we would ever return to business as usual.

While pandemic protocols have now mostly been phased out in workplaces, the most enduring long-term change is likely to be a switch to a hybrid model of remote working. Many people will work from home for a few days a week, virtual meetings will be more common and the office reserved for business best done in person such as negotiations, brainstorming, critical decisions and discussions involving sensitive feedback. It is quite likely emotion AI will be increasingly seen as the answer to shaping and monitoring our drastically changing and fragmented modern workplace.

Ignore for a moment any mistrust of the machines. This massive shift in working practices, which is at last being recognised and widely talked about, without a doubt presents a once-in-a-lifetime opportunity to reconsider the workplace.

You may well be one of the many millions who saw the pandemic as a full-stop. A moment to pause and consider, 'Am I happy in my job?' If the response was no, your solution might have been to try something new, but what if you didn't do that? What if, instead of starting a whole new career, you and I and everyone else used this opportunity to work together to make our existing workplaces what they should be?

If we put our minds to it, we could create a more innovative, engaging environment where everyone feels able to bring their full selves to work. If you are in a position of leadership, you could play an important part in creating a better workplace for everyone.

Employees have for so long been asking for more from those who lead them. Leaders and managers have a new chance to meet those demands, engage their employees and make better workplaces. The key to this is for organisations to switch from simply managing emotions to finally moving towards recognising and accepting the importance of emotion in the workplace.

Emotions are not just something we need to be aware of. A strategy of greater emotional openness is key to successful leadership. It is what organisation leaders need to inspire others to help us all deliver. For employees, it answers their burning need to express themselves and be honest about their views.

A strategy to understand and embrace emotions is no longer a nice-to-have. In an increasingly complex world, with ever greater use of technology, it is the key to attracting and retaining talent, fostering healthy and happy work environments, and maintaining productivity.

Summary

This chapter has looked at the importance of being open to understanding and embracing emotions at work. An employer who considers and works with the emotions of their humanforce will benefit from not only engaged and settled team members, but also increased productivity, efficiency and profits. The old saying 'a happy workforce is a productive workforce' isn't just an empty cliché, but it's time to take it one step further and consider the true concept of a humanforce. At the heart of being human is emotion.

TWO

The Power Of Emotion

For many centuries, the prevailing view was that emotions are illogical, maybe even a little crazy, and for the most part best disregarded. No doubt this was the foundation for the various dismissive phrases that are still a firm part of our language today.

The Ancient Greeks called emotions *pathē*, which means experience or suffering, with the clear implication that reasoned, logical thinking has a much higher value. Plato said that *pathē* were disturbances in our soul that knocked us off balance and disrupted our calm.[1] Aristotle, on the other hand, said emotions were largely passive states.[2] He did, however, believe they could be expertly used to win any persuasive argument.

Fast forward to the nineteenth century and Charles Darwin established what is called a functional view of emotion.[3] The English naturalist, geologist and biologist pioneered the idea that emotions signal valuable information and energise adaptive behaviour, which is central to survival. Feelings of love and affection lead people to seek out mates and reproduce. Fear compels us to either fight or flee the source of danger. Emotions motivate us to respond quickly and adapt to changes in our environment, which is key to our chances of success and survival.

Darwin's theories encouraged others to consider how emotions and moods play an essential role in thought processes, influencing our judgement and behaviour. When scientists began to study different regions of the brain, they questioned how emotions interact with our thinking and subsequent actions. Many concluded that emotions are basically electro-chemical signals that flow through our body. They're released in our brain in response to our perceptions about the world around us and we experience hundreds of emotions all the time, even though we are not always aware of it.

This train of thought led researchers to question the difference between, say, an emotion and a feeling or an emotion and behaviour. What comes first? Is it emotions, with the feelings following on after the emotion chemicals go to work in our bodies? Is that what will produce a subsequent mood or behaviour?

The theories

Several differing theories appeared in quick succession in the twentieth century. While not all of them entirely agreed with each other, a consensus emerged: emotion, feeling, thought and behaviour are all closely linked. Today, researchers and scientists often define emotions as a multi-part response to situations that we perceive as being important and relevant to our goals.

Walter Cannon and Philip Bard arguably kicked this off by developing the Cannon-Bard theory, suggesting that we experience physiological reactions linked to emotions without feeling them.[4] More specifically, emotions result when messages are sent to our brain in response to a stimulus, leading to a physical reaction.

I see a lion → I am afraid → My heart starts racing → I run away.

According to the Cannon-Bard theory of emotion, we react to a stimulus and experience the associated emotion at the exact same time. Thus, if we are starting a new job, the first day will be stressful. There are new co-workers to meet, senior staff to impress, meetings to attend, not to mention finding our way around the place. We will feel the emotional and physical signs of stress – nervousness and the sensation of butterflies in our stomach – simultaneously.

The Schachter-Singer theory, which followed Cannon-Bard, takes a similar yet subtly different approach.[5] This cognitive theory suggests that the physiological arousal comes first, and then we identify the reason for this arousal before labelling it as an emotion. In other words, the experience of emotion comes first, and then we have the emotional response.

I see a lion → My heart is racing and I am trembling → My rapid heart rate and trembling are caused by fear → I am scared.

The Cognitive Appraisal Theory, also known as the Lazarus Theory of Emotion after the person who developed it, Richard Lazarus, is broadly similar.[6] According to this theory, first there's a stimulus, followed by a thought, which then leads to physical response and emotion. If you were to encounter that lion, the sequence of events would be:

I see a lion → Oh no, I am in danger → I am scared → My heart starts racing.

A consensus has evolved that emotions are like chemicals that are released in a fraction of a second in response to a trigger. If, say, a dog is snarling at you or a friend is telling you a sad story, it triggers emotions of fear or sadness to be released.

It takes our brain a quarter of a second to identify the trigger and another quarter of a second to produce the chemical which goes all around our body in a sort of feedback loop between that and our brain. It is interesting to note that our emotions, when worked with, do not last long. According to Harvard brain scientist Dr Jill Bolte Taylor, ninety seconds is all it takes to identify an emotion and allow it to dissipate.[7]

As we digest and integrate the emotion, it leads to a feeling. This is a physical sensation in the body such as a sore tummy or a lump in our throat or a chill. This physical sensation will arrive very quickly and may feel like it is triggered at almost the same time as an emotion. It's actually our body that is giving us the clue that we're having an emotion.

Finally, we will experience a mood. A mood is what results from the mixture of feelings and emotions, and it can go on for some time, even throughout the day. Our behaviour will be affected, depending on how we deal with the emotion. Certainly, if we don't deal with the emotion or push it away, or don't acknowledge what's happening, then our mood could be affected far longer than it needs to be, as will our behaviour. It is worth noting here that our mood can be influenced by other factors, too, such as the environment or what we've been eating.

Thus, to return to our lion:

I see a lion → I feel fear → I am moving away from it because if I don't, I might be eaten.

There is an emotion, a thought, a feeling in our body such as panic or a difficulty breathing, and then we'll do something: a behaviour.

Another significant event in this period that enhanced our understanding of emotions was in the seventies when psychologist Paul Ekman articulated six basic or primary emotions.[8] By this stage, there was a greater understanding that there were many different types of emotions that influence how we live and interact with others, dictating our choices and actions. It was, however, Ekman who identified six emotions that are universally experienced across all cultures: happiness, sadness, disgust, fear, surprise and anger. He later expanded that list to include pride, shame, embarrassment and excitement.

Thoughts on what emotions should be included in this list have varied over the years. Ekman noted that people from diverse cultures differ in the way they display and express emotion. There are also distinct variations in our response to specific events, depending upon where we were born and brought up. What provokes you into anger may not make someone from elsewhere angry, but the universal emotion of anger is the same. Likewise, the language we use to express our emotions differs depending upon where we are, as does the number of words we have to express each one.

The Germans have the wonderful word *schaden-freude* to describe the pleasure we get when we hear an enemy has undergone a misfortune. No doubt people around the world experience something similar, but in most languages, including English, there is no equivalent word.

Emotions are universal, but when I train in corporate settings, I just focus on four: happiness, sadness, fear and anger. These are the easiest ones for people to recognise, but the acknowledgement of the main types of emotions is crucial in gaining a deep understanding of how they are expressed and the impact they might have on our behaviour.

Every emotion has its purpose

Dr Rebecca Nicholson, Author, Researcher and Strategist, The Conflict Doctor

Emotions are the number-one driver of conflict. They tell us what's important to us and what our drivers are. They tell us what we feel strongly about or that something is wrong or that our boundaries have been violated. In my work in conflict, emotion is usually the primary indicator something needs to be dealt with.

When you understand your emotions, drives and ambitions and what makes you angry, it puts you in a place where you are able to resolve the conflict more effectively. Likewise, the more you understand about your own emotions and how they drive you, the more you will understand about how others are driven by their emotions. Knowing how they tick will give you a lot of options when you're weighing up how to work with people or motivate them.

Emotions are *meant* to be felt, but somehow, we do a good job of suppressing the ones we don't like. The reason for this is that we don't relish the unpleasant feelings that they produce. We don't like the knot in our stomach or the way our heart races. We prefer to feel relaxed and calm.

Earlier, I introduced the analogy that emotions are like email messages which we can choose to open and deal with, or ignore. While it is natural to avoid any emotions that we believe might challenge us or give us pain, they are simply a message prompting us to take an action which will deal with the message.

Let's take as an example the core messages behind some emotions that we mostly try to avoid.

Emotion	Message	Prompt
Anger	One of my values has not been respected or something is unjust or unfair	I need to draw a boundary or repair what is wrong
Fear	There is danger or something is unsafe	I need to protect myself
Sadness	I have lost something that is important to me	I need to accept it and let go

The core messages behind common emotions

Often, emotions like those in the table above are extremely powerful. If we ignore them or fail to open up these messages, they will remain in our inbox to bug us. Hour by hour, they will drain our energy and stop us from being our best selves. These emotions do not disappear; they remain stuck in our bodies for days, weeks or much longer.

When we suppress our emotions, it can lead to compensation behaviours such as excessive eating or drinking, or we may disconnect by isolating or withdrawing. As well as impacting our own health, it can have a negative impact on those closest to us.

To put this into context, think about a moment when you experienced a strong unpleasant emotion at work. Perhaps a colleague interrupted you in a meeting or someone spoke to you in a disrespectful way. Reflect upon how you felt at that time and identify the emotions that were present. Perhaps you experienced frustration, anger or sadness. What was it that anger was telling you? What was behind the sadness?

Once you step back and consider what might be behind the emotion, it helps you decide how to work with your emotions and choose the appropriate course of action. We will talk more about this process in the next chapter.

What about pleasant emotions such as joy, excitement, gratitude? These are good and necessary, and we need to work to maintain these emotions as they give us energy and help us to flourish.

There has been a lot of work done in this field. Dr Martin Seligman, who is well known in the field of positive psychology, has developed a model setting out the five building blocks which enable people to flourish, cultivate their talents, build relationships and contribute meaningfully to the world.[9] One of these building blocks is positive emotions. Dr Seligman says when we look at our past and there is contentment in that past, it cultivates gratitude and forgiveness, which in turn translate to happiness in the present.

Barbara L Fredrickson PhD, a leading scholar within social psychology, affective science and positive psychology, has been studying and advancing the science of positive emotions for more than twenty years.[10] She has identified the ten most important pleasant emotions, which are: joy, gratitude, serenity, interest, hope, pride, amusement, inspiration, awe and love.

There has been much written about the role of positive emotions at work and their benefits have been well documented. Studies show their impact on health, as well as in building trust, combatting depression and helping people to recover from stress. Fredrickson's research shows that the difference between people who are flourishing and those who aren't lies in how much positive emotion they are able to self-generate from pleasant everyday activities such as social interactions, learning and helping others. She likens positive emotions to nutrients which, even if only experienced on a temporary basis, influence how our brain works, making us more flexible while impacting our personal resilience and resourcefulness.

The emotion of gratitude has been shown to have a significant impact on physical and mental wellbeing, with one study suggesting it can reduce the risks associated with heart failure.[11] Another study shows that practising gratitude eases symptoms of anxiety and depression.[12] Meanwhile, a bit of good old-fashioned laughter lowers levels of cortisol to reduce the risk of heart attacks.[13] We will look in more detail at the benefits of positive emotions later on.

However, there can be a downside to too many happy emotions. You might know someone who always seems to be positive and joyful. They are relentlessly cheerful and never complain. You can be certain that they *work* at this positivity.

You might ask, 'What could possibly be the downside of this positivity?' My immediate response is that it may be a way for these people to hide or mask their real emotions. While they may be good at avoiding unpleasant feelings and have techniques to steer towards the happy ones, they are not always in touch with reality.

The same can be said for workplaces that focus vast amounts of attention on happy emotions such as joy, inspiration and contentment. Experts call it 'positivity bias'. The problem with positivity bias is that, if pushed too far, it can become toxic. It can lead people to avoid problems and miss warning signs for the business.

Happiness and being enduringly positive are endlessly portrayed as a good thing, but be aware that positivity bias may be a way of avoiding the difficult emotions and facing reality. We look more at the problems with toxic positivity in Chapter Nine.

Emotions have a message and we cannot ignore them, but how much can we show in the workplace? How much of each emotion is enough? When does it become too much? Even though each emotion has a crucial message, their combined intensity can be unhelpful at times and this is why we need to regulate them.

I go on to discuss the regulation of emotions in the next chapter of this book. For now, let's concentrate on their power.

Emotional power at work

To start the process of creating a better workplace, we need to gain an understanding of the value of emotions and our emotional response at work. There are so many different demands upon us in our careers today. We need to be continually learning; we need to be creative; we need to be innovative; and we need to make good decisions, particularly if we are in any sort of position of leadership. We also need to manage our relationships with our colleagues. Our emotions have an impact in each one of these areas.

Before looking in Chapter Three at what adjustments we might make to our emotions to create a better workplace and get the best out of everyone, let's look at some main areas where emotions play a key role.

Learning

Emotions influence how we learn because they are inherently linked to cognitive skills such as attention, memory, executive function, decision making, critical thinking, problem solving and regulation. Emotions such as joy, excitement and passion will motivate us to learn. They activate the reward system of the brain, making learning desirable, and aid in focus and attention. Positive emotional states can help us to broaden our perspective, see alternatives, persist through challenges and respond positively to criticism or failure, but certain emotional states such as stress inhibit our ability to learn.

Without a doubt, chronic stress has a powerful influence on our emotions. Many workers report feeling exhausted, negative and isolated, the classic signs of chronic stress and burnout. As well as impacting us on a personal basis, stress and anxiety can inhibit our ability to learn and therefore progress in our careers.

There is a huge amount to get to grips with today. The workplace many of us returned to post-pandemic is different to before. Even before the pandemic, there had been a huge shift towards digital. This was accelerated manyfold during the crisis and there is now a much faster adoption of automation, AI and online working. This will transform many jobs, some almost unrecognisably, meaning we need to learn many new working practices. The irony is, the stress about these changes and how we adapt to them may inhibit people from giving them their best shot.

STUDY: We feel, therefore we learn[14]

Learning, attention, memory and decision making, areas which we have relied on to develop our knowledge since we first entered the school system, are profoundly affected by and subsumed within the processes of emotional thought. This study of brain-damaged patients supports this hypothesis, suggesting an *emotional rudder* is required to steer how we absorb skills and knowledge, and guide judgement and action.

Creativity

In today's uncertain world, creativity is ranked as a vital skill because it gives a business the edge in addressing challenges and opportunities. Indeed, a workplace survey focusing on 50,000 different skills identified creativity as *the* most important, essential to compete in the modern marketplace, ranking it above management, integrity and vision.[15] Businesses that invest in creativity are more likely to be competitive, to provide a better customer experience, to be financially successful and, most importantly, to have happier employees than those that don't.

Unfortunately, creativity is something that a lot of companies struggle with, and wouldn't you know it? Emotions play a key role here because energy-sapping emotions such as anger and fear can inhibit creativity.

Let's look at one of these emotions, fear, to see how it might squash a person's inspiration. Imagine a creative employee who has been charged with coming up with a brilliant new concept to adapt to a change in the market.

Before they even start, they already know that they face several fear pinch points. They've got to come up with the ground-breaking idea. Then, they're going to have to present it to the boss. There's always the inevitable delay while the boss takes their sweet time to evaluate the idea. After that, there will be the dreaded feedback session. Anticipating that is never nice, particularly if a boss is known not to mince their words. If the idea is not 100% right, it is back to the drawing board with the prospect of starting the whole cycle again. Rinse and repeat. It is no wonder that processes like this inhibit future creativity.

If people don't feel safe to come up with a suggestion or to express a new idea without it being shot down or to try something and fail, then creativity is out the window. Emotions such as fear are an absolute inhibitor to creativity.

Many firms have sought to circumvent the cycle of fear and other energy-sapping emotions by focusing on creating environments that encourage a free flow of energy. You know the sort of thing: chill-out pods, bean bags and ping-pong tables. While it all sounds very nice, you may be surprised to hear that too much energy doesn't necessarily make for the ultimate in creativity.

As it happens, one of the most productive states of all is boredom. John Eastwood, a psychologist at the boredom lab at York University in Canada, says that when we're bored, we're stuck.[16] Our mental capacities are low, but at the same time, we're itching to engage our mind. This makes us become considerably more creative.

We certainly saw evidence of this during the pandemic. People were fed up and listless during successive lockdowns and that prompted us to be more creative. We cooked, danced, drew, painted and invented new board games, all because we were given time and space to express ourselves.

As evidenced by the study below, feeling down also contributes to our flurry of creativity.

STUDY: The upside of feeling down[17]

Joe Forgas found that while positive moods do indeed promote creativity, flexibility and co-operation, sadness can also make us focused and diligent. In fact, research by this psychology professor suggests that being miserable can at times actually improve our creative performance.

In this study, a random selection of customers leaving a corner shop were asked how many unusual objects they remembered seeing on the counter. The conditions were carefully controlled, with the same store, the same time of day, the same checkout operator and the same placements of the unusual objects. The only difference was the weather as the customers exited the shop. The researchers found that people performed much better on the memory test when the weather was unpleasant and they were in a slightly negative mood. When they emerged into sunlight, feeling happy and carefree, they could barely remember any of the objects.

Decision making

Decision making is an integral part of work, even for those who are not in a leadership position. Our ability to make the right choices has an impact on our careers, as well as the success of our employers. Thus, it is important that we are effective decision makers. Get it right and we can save time and resources, gain the respect of others, improve productivity and prevent mistakes. Consequently, it makes sense to fully understand the process so that we can maintain and, better still, improve our decision-making skills.

When it comes to decisions, most of us consider that it is our rational brain or mental power that does the heavy lifting. Getting it right is all down to our intelligence, but think about it again. Does emotion play a role in that? The answer is unequivocally, yes, it does. You may just never have considered it in this way before.

Lots of people talk about 'going with my gut' or using their intuition. They take an action because it 'just feels right'. This is a perfect example of emotion determining our actions. Often these emotion-based decisions are, on face value, entirely irrational, contradicting all the evidence. If, say, we fear flying, we will drive to a destination, even though statistically, driving is more dangerous than flying.

Similarly, if we are feeling positive, confident and happy, we'll most likely reach a conclusion about something in one way. We might come to a completely different conclusion if we're feeling angry, sad or unhappy.

Our emotions really do determine a lot of what we do. We think it's our brain power or our rationalising. It isn't.

STUDY: The influence of teacher emotion on grading practices[18]

In an experiment, teachers were divided into two groups. One group was told to write about a positive classroom experience, while the other was assigned to recall a negative memory. Then, they were all asked to grade the same essay from students. The group that had previously recorded their positive experiences marked the essay a full grade higher than the group that had focused on negative thoughts.

Later, when the teachers were asked if they believed their mood affected how they evaluated the papers, 87% of them said no, it didn't have any impact. The scores seem to indicate otherwise.

Even though we know that emotions impact our decision making, we should be wary of making simplistic assumptions. While positive thoughts put the teachers in the study in a good frame of mind, it doesn't follow that we will always make the best decisions because we are happy. If we are experiencing strong energy-draining emotions, such as anxiety, anger and sadness, we may be cautious about making decisions, taking time to weigh the facts carefully. Conversely, if we're in a more positive frame of mind, we may be more impetuous and impulsive, and inclined to forget facts in favour of going with our gut.

The book *Thinking, Fast and Slow* by Nobel Prize winner Daniel Kahneman sheds some welcome light on this.[19] As the title suggests, Kahneman says we have two systems of thinking: a fast system and a slow system. We use the slow system when we need to really analyse and do some heavy thinking for the big calls such as buying a house. The fast system, on the other hand, is deployed almost unconsciously for stuff we don't need to give much thought to, such as deciding whether to eat the last bit of chocolate or to put our toe in the water at the seaside. The fast system, where we make decisions and take actions within fractions of a second, is akin to what we believe to be our gut-based moves.

Thus, our brains are working on two separate but overlapping tracks. One responds without much or any deliberation, and the other takes its time and weighs the information first. The quick decisions that we make are susceptible to our moods, emotions and biases.

While it is not something we can manage, we are not utterly helpless in this. Anyone who needs to make a decision or a number of decisions during the day can actively focus on their emotional wellbeing.

Say, for example, Claire has an argument with her partner before work and starts her commute feeling unhappy. She needs to acknowledge to herself what has happened and that, unless she does something to regulate herself, the likelihood is that her unhappiness will have an impact on her decisions during the day. It may also impact how she behaves with her colleagues.

Motivation and engagement

Motivation is a big deal at work. Many businesses spend a fortune on measures to keep their employees motivated, with variable results. Gallup's 2021 worldwide survey on motivation found that only 15%

of employees are motivated.[20] In Europe, only 10% of employees are motivated at work, compared to 33% in the US. The employee motivation statistics for the UK are even more alarming, with the number as low as 8%. This represents a noticeable decrease over the years too, indicating motivation remains a massive challenge for all organisations.

What, though, do we mean by motivation? Interestingly, the word motivation is closely connected to the word emotion. Indeed, the Latin root for the word emotion is *emovere*, meaning to move, excite or motivate. Our emotions motivate us, move us, energise us and help us make sense of everything we experience.

Motivation is a driving force that initiates and impacts our behaviour, and we follow our motivations because they make us feel good and rewarded. Motivation is not the same as engagement, although both have a huge impact on business performance, and both are impacted by emotional connection. Engagement describes a sense of purpose, belonging and commitment to an organisation, whereas motivation is the willpower and drive to act upon those feelings. Engagement serves as the foundation for employees to do their best work, while motivation is the fuel or energy they require to actually do it. When employee engagement is high, factors such as pride in the organisation, leadership, diversity, health and wellbeing, and purpose will be high also.

There are lots of different models we can use to analyse what motivates us at work, with one of the best known being the Maslow Hierarchy of Needs. In his 1943 paper *A Theory of Human Motivation*,[21] Abraham Maslow identified five needs: physiological (food and clothing), safety (job security), love and belonging (friendship), esteem and self-actualisation. Starting with physiological, each one needs to be satisfied in turn before individuals can attend to the next one on the list.

Maslow's pyramid is very well known, but it has been challenged for not being based on research. In recent years, expert research has increasingly pinpointed another crucial factor in motivation: the need to be connected. We all want to feel like we are attached to something and to have a feeling of belonging.

A study of 25,000 leaders for the book *The Inspiring Leader* discovered that those who were most inspiring (the top 10% of the group) had something unique in common: their ability to establish a strong emotional connection with their employees.[22] Our ability to connect with our teams, peers and bosses as humans with emotions brings out the best in them.

To achieve attachment and belonging in the workplace, we need to involve emotions. People need to feel they are in a place where there is human connection, love, warmth and emotion. In a workplace that clamps down on emotions, people are not going to feel connected. They won't feel that motivating attachment of belonging to something. Belonging, connection, love and warmth are all explored in more detail in Part Three of this book.

Health and wellbeing

The toll the pandemic had on all our lives was evident as we emerged from it. On a daily basis, I coached and worked with many individuals who were suffering from mental-health issues and finding it hard to recover their motivation.

Research quite rightly points to the fact that health and wellbeing at work should be a top priority for all employers as they look ahead to new ways of working and navigate a changed business world. More than half the workforce (57%) say they're fed up and might quit. This goes all the way to the top too, with 76% of C-Suite executives agreeing that the pandemic has impacted their overall health.[23]

The post-pandemic wellbeing slump was felt keenly around the world. Europe and South Asia saw wellbeing down 5% since 2021, with workers reporting feeling that their current life was worse than before the pandemic and hopes for the future were bleak.[24] Perhaps the most alarming figure here is that the number of employees who feel that their employer cares about their wellbeing is 24%.[25]

When employers fail to address work-related stress, it leads to burnout, defined as a state of physical and emotional exhaustion. Burnout has a profound effect on us, mentally and physically, and when left untreated can cause real long-term mental-health issues including exhaustion, depression and anxiety, and lead to diseases and physical-health conditions such as cancer, diabetes and metabolic syndromes.

Stress is a word that is often used in the context of health and wellbeing, and many of my clients have asked me whether it can be classed as an emotion. My response is that it is a feeling of physical, mental or emotional tension caused by events that provoke emotions such as fear and anger. When we are stressed, it is our body's reaction to a challenge or a demand.

A little stress in itself is not a bad thing. It focuses us, motivates us and, over time, it helps us to evolve. At work, it helps us to meet deadlines or find solutions to complex problems. The difficulty arises if we are in a state of constant stress over a long period of time. This is what we call chronic stress. Chronic stress can make it challenging for us to slow down, focus our attention and learn something new.

Almost everyone will be familiar with the signs of workplace stress. If I can't go to sleep at night, I know that there's a problem and I can be certain that it's to do with my emotions, which can often be traced back to my job. It's the same if I don't have any appetite and skip meals. What I have often found when working with my clients is that many have been surviving on automatic pilot, unaware of what might be happening to them, while others may have an idea, but choose to ignore what their emotions are trying to tell them.

Let me give you a little background to what is going on inside us all and explain some of the science behind our reactions. What happens when we face a challenge or threat?

Say, for example, you are asked to deliver the results of a project to a senior leadership team and you have never presented at this level before, or perhaps you are promoted to a leadership role for the first time. Neither scenario is life threatening, but will inevitably provoke the same emotions and physical sensations.

The prefrontal cortex and amygdala are the key regions of the brain involved with our physiological and behavioural responses to stress and fear. The prefrontal cortex is there to make rational decisions and the amygdala is in the unconscious part of the brain. External stimuli, from sight, hearing, touch, smell and taste, activate a number of regions of the brain, including the amygdala, and provoke the fight, flight, freeze response. This prevents us from accessing our prefrontal cortex to help us react in a more rational, reasoned way.

The process dates back to our ancestors who needed to be able to run or go into battle just to survive. Today, most of us do not face the same dangerous situations on a daily basis, yet our bodies are still wired in the same way. Therefore, we need to be able to find a way to adjust our response. Sure, if we are in a situation where there is an actual imminent physical threat, then the fight or, probably more prudently, flight response can be life-saving. However, if we are simply stressed when trying to figure out how to deal with a new role, the fight, flight or freeze impulse can seriously interfere with what we want to do.

During times of stress, our bodies release cortisol, a stress hormone that helps us to stay alert and endure. Initially, the cortisol has a good function and helps us to maintain our performance during challenging times, but if it is not moderated over time, levels will rise in the body and become toxic. If we have consistently high levels of cortisol, our bodies can become used to having too much in our blood, which can lead to inflammation and a weakened immune system.

High cortisol levels also act to reduce hormones that could have a positive impact. Feel-good hormones such as serotonin and dopamine, a pleasure hormone related to motivation, will go down when we experience too much stress. Overall, this will upset our hormone balance, deplete the brain chemicals required for happiness and damage the immune system.

Persistently chronic levels of stress can contribute to a variety of short-term ailments such as headaches, backache and skin problems. They can also lead to long-term problems including:

- High blood pressure

- Heart disease

- Dehydration

- Insomnia

- Compromised immune system

- Diabetes

- Digestive issues

Too much stress will impair not just the body, but the mind too. Our brains are as much a part of our body as anything else and our emotions impact the functioning of our brain.

Research has shown what happens to our brains during prolonged periods of stress. Stress causes a deterioration of brain regions, which impacts cognitive functions. Working memory, attention, response inhibition and cognitive flexibility have all been found to be impaired by stress.[26] At work, this could translate into a reduced ability to concentrate, control impulses, remember and plan.

One study gave participants a stress test where they were asked to improvise a ten-minute speech in front of an audience.[27] Their ability to remember and plan was reduced after the test compared to beforehand, leading to the conclusion that stress hindered their performance. Another study reported that high blood levels of the stress hormone cortisol are associated with memory impairments and smaller brain volumes in young and middle-aged adults.[28]

STUDY: The psychological impact of quarantine and how to reduce it[29]

A study of the psychological effects of quarantine during COVID-19 found post-traumatic stress symptoms, as well as confusion and anger. Stress caused by prolonged quarantine durations produced emotional reactions to fear of infection, frustration, boredom and loneliness. What is interesting is the study also showed these effects were long-lasting, enduring even after quarantine had ended. They revealed far-reaching long-term consequences stretching beyond the psychological to physical and mental disorders.

Burnout is not something that happens overnight. It is a slow, insidious process where people are not able to deal with the chronic stress they feel at work. Eventually, it overwhelms them.

There are many ways to reduce chronic stress and there is much that an individual can do to look after their personal health and wellbeing. Indeed, many companies today offer resilience or health and wellbeing training to their employees to arm them with tips and tools to manage their stress. Even so, I have been frustrated at how company leaders too often see the issue of burnout as an individual problem, which can be solved with training, yoga, sport and other personal resilience techniques.

Of course, employees do have to look after their health and wellbeing, but mounting evidence from studies shifts the responsibility for burnout on to organisations themselves. At HumanForce, we train managers to understand that the causes of burnout do not just lie with the individual and are often a result of a poor emotional culture and weak leadership.

Burnout can be triggered by a number of organisational factors such as a heavy workload, a lack of reward or recognition, a perceived lack of fairness across teams and mismatched values between employer and employee. The most effective way to address chronic stress in the workplace is to have a comprehensive systemic approach.

Assessing the health of employees and identifying the organisational factors that could be contributing to chronic stress or ill health is the first step. This is followed by a strategy to address all of this, which could include a mixture of policies, practices, leadership training and other preventative support and guidance for all employees. Above all, toxic workplace behaviour must be addressed. For me, this is the key to improved health at work. Organisations must build emotional cultures that are supportive, caring and inclusive.

Summary

This chapter has covered a lot, starting with the history and theories about emotions that have coloured the thinking on this fascinating subject over the centuries. We've looked at what emotions really are and why it's important not to ignore them, even the ones that cause unpleasant sensations such as racing heart or churning stomach. Along the way, I have shared some expert opinions and referenced pertinent research and studies.

THREE
Working With Emotions

Life is good. That project you've been worried about is now definitely on track. Earlier this week, the team leader singled you out for praise during the group briefing. There's a strong chance that you'll soon get the promotion you have long coveted. The money will come in handy, but it is more than that. It'll mean you are being recognised for your skill and hard work.

Suddenly, without warning, your mood sinks. You feel bad tempered and thoroughly fed up. Tasks which used to motivate and excite you now seem like a chore. What is going on?

If this scenario feels in any way familiar, take a look around you. What is the general mood among the people with whom you work most closely? There is a high chance that someone on the team, maybe even a few colleagues, are in a foul mood or hate their job or feel thoroughly disengaged, or all of the above.

Emotions are contagious. As human beings, we synchronise with the emotions of those around us, either consciously or subconsciously. At the most basic level, we mimic the expressions, vocalisations and movements of those we are with. When we see people laugh, we tend to laugh too. Unfortunately, bad moods are even more potent. When those around us are angry and frustrated with their lot, we start to feel the same.

In the previous chapter, we looked at all the reasons why it is important to bring our best self to work. A positive mindset can enhance our creativity and learning. It can help us make better decisions and keep us motivated, even during the most challenging times. It even has an impact on our health and wellbeing.

There is, however, another important reason to work with our emotions: they have an impact upon everyone around us. If we are constantly angry or resentful or disengaged, it sets off a ripple effect that can bring down the whole team.

I, like most people, have had first-hand experience of this. I worked closely with a colleague who would routinely bring all her emotions to work, good and bad, but mostly bad. Sometimes, she didn't even turn up because, as she would later tell us, she felt too emotionally overwhelmed.

Even though I tried to shrug it off, it took a huge toll on me, and I know my colleagues felt the impact too. Every time this colleague was in the office, it felt like all the air was being sucked out of the room. While I would be the first to wholeheartedly encourage emotions in the workplace, we need to work with them, respecting the needs and feelings of others.

By working with emotions, we will not only feel better, but we'll also be better people at work based on the impact we have on those around us. This is not a strategy to avoid or suppress emotions. What we're aiming for is to put ourselves in a position of choice. We will choose how we work with and respond to an emotion to be able to achieve our goals.

The steps to emotional health

Before we look at some tools to work with emotions, there is something that needs to be said. We must be willing to welcome *all* emotions, pleasant and unpleasant, accepting them as they arise.

Acceptance of emotions is key in emotional work. It does not mean *tolerating* your emotions or *enduring* them or *giving in* to them. It is about making room for what shows up in the moment, even if it is unpleasant and you may not like the experience. Accepting or welcoming emotions is about being willing to feel them in your body and being open to the message that they bring. In this way, you can take action to move forward. Above all, you waste no valuable energy in trying to suppress or avoid those emotions.

We have already seen what can happen if we choose not to welcome certain emotions and instead suppress or ignore them. This chapter sets out how acceptance can unfold and the tools that we can use to work with our emotions more effectively.

Working with emotions requires a sequential multi-stage approach which begins with us becoming aware of our emotions, moves us on to understanding what they are trying to tell us, and then on to deciding whether or not to do something about them. It is the process of getting to know our own emotions and how we relate to others. Some describe this process as becoming an 'emotional scientist', but I prefer 'emotional detective'.

STUDY: The process model of emotion regulation[1]

Psychologist James Gross, one of the leading figures in the field of emotional regulation, assumes that emotions are reactions to the world, so if we want to feel differently, we need to change the way we think or pay attention to events, anticipating and preparing for them. For example, anyone afraid of large groups should avoid situations where there are lots of people because that will trigger their fear. Alternatively, if the circumstances can't be changed, the person should change what they *mean* to them or adopt distraction techniques. The goal is to master emotions, steering them to materialise, or not, at just the right time.

Gross's model sets out strategies to regulate and control emotions before anything happens. Some of the key strategies he suggests we deploy include:

Situational selection: consciously selecting situations that are less likely to lead to emotion regulation problems. For example, adults with attention deficit hyperactivity disorder (ADHD) who seek to be around those who legitimise rather than stigmatise their problems are actively engaging in situational selection. Similarly, they will seek out ADHD-friendly work environments, putting themselves in situations they know are not going to cause them problems.

Situation modification: where we modify situations that trigger emotional problems. Children and teenagers who sit themselves away from a classmate who is dangerous or a known bully are modifying the situation to their own benefit to avoid being exposed to unpleasant behaviour. In the workplace, we may avoid members of the team who exhibit toxic behaviour.

Attention deployment: the strategic deployment of our attention to distract it from the source of an emotional problem. A good example of this is an experiment carried out with a group of four-year-olds who were given a marshmallow and told that if they waited for fifteen minutes before eating it, they'd receive a second one.[2] Half of the group managed it and half of them didn't. The children who didn't give in to temptation successfully controlled themselves by singing songs, walking around the room or even covering their eyes. These are all classic attention deployment techniques.

Each of Gross's tactics is useful in preventing strong emotions arising and being potentially damaging, but

he is not saying that emotions can be entirely eliminated. They can't and we shouldn't try to do so. It is
inevitable that emotions, even strong ones, will arise.
Then the challenge will be how to *respond* to emotions
rather than react to them.

The first step in working with emotions is awareness and paying attention. This is illustrated by the
classic definition of EQ depicted in a simple grid.

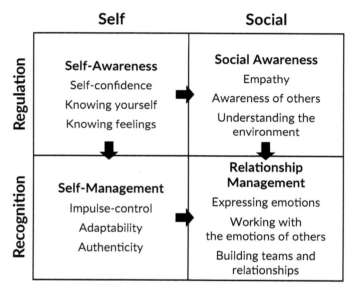

Daniel Goleman's framework of EQ[3]

As the grid shows, this process begins with awareness
of self and our own emotions as they happen, before
moving on to managing our emotions to direct our
behaviour positively. Stage two is to correctly perceive
and understand emotions in others before we move
on to managing our interaction with those people.

The first step, self-awareness, depends on our ability to recognise our emotions and examine them objectively. Many of us find this hard, especially if we're running around 24/7 like a hamster on a wheel. There just never seems to be enough time to pause and pay attention; or perhaps more accurately, we don't give ourselves time.

I've lost count of the number of clients who tell me they are under pressure from the time they start work in the morning to the moment they arrive home. In fact, most of them say they continue to feel under pressure even after they close their front door behind them. They find it impossible to step back, let alone take stock of their emotions.

The danger with this always-on culture is that emotions are in the driving seat. They are managing us rather than the other way around. Our knee-jerk response to events is dictated by the limbic brain rather than the neocortex, which is the rational or thinking part of our brain.

To understand the ramifications, take as an example an unfortunate event such as your car failing to start ahead of the morning commute. Immediately, you will be hit by strong emotions. A knot of tension will appear in your stomach because it is now inevitable that you are going to be late for work. Your throat may tighten as you mentally list everything you had planned that will now need to be pushed back or even shelved altogether.

The anxiety might well push you into an instinctive reaction as your mind races through the alternative means of getting to work rather than prioritising a call to the garage to arrange repairs (thus possibly throwing the rest of the week into chaos). After a dash for the train, you arrive an hour later than intended, so rush through meetings to catch up. Your tension levels are now so high, you don't even notice how brusque you're being with colleagues. Throughout the day, all your decisions are made at break-neck speed with far less of your usual meticulous scrutiny. It's highly likely by the end of the day that, as well as offending numerous colleagues and infecting the office with your irritable mood, you will have made many mistakes.

What could you have done differently?

When an unexpected event like this happens and you are immediately flooded with physical feelings, make a conscious decision to step back and pause. Say to yourself, 'OK, yes, I'm late and I am worried about catching up, but I am going to take a deep breath. I am going to give myself time to decide how to react to this event rather than doing so on automatic pilot.'

Imagine how different things would have been if you had consciously paused on that morning when the car didn't start and made a choice about how to react to that event. You wouldn't have rushed through meetings or been unpleasant to colleagues or opened yourself up to making errors. Your car would already be in the garage being fixed, too.

When you allow the limbic brain to take control and ultimately override any logic or reason, you will act impulsively and not necessarily in your best interests.

Think of all the times your limbic brain has taken control at work. Consider your response when a senior colleague yelled at you or criticised your work, or a member of the team mocked you. You may have shouted back or walked out of the room, or even started to cry. None of these reactions are appropriate.

Once again, reflect upon how the outcome might have been different if you had paused and given yourself time to react with a considered and conscious response. Giving yourself space to respond might only take a few seconds, but it will completely change the outcome.

In the rest of the chapter, we will go through a sequence of techniques and tools you can use to give yourself that space. They will take practice and are not something that you can master instantly, or even overnight. For some people, this process will come more naturally than for others, who may even find it a little uncomfortable at first. In the same way as you have to keep trying over and over when learning any new skill, you will need to commit to working at these techniques.

Tool #1 – Pay attention

When I introduce the term 'mindfulness' to groups I work with, there is often a certain amount of cynicism. The scornful response is something along the lines of: 'Isn't that just lying down in a dark room for forty-five minutes, thinking about stuff?' It can be, but doesn't have to be.

Mindfulness is paying attention to an experience on a moment-to-moment basis in an open and non-judgmental way. It helps us to connect to how we are, reduces stress and gives us space to make a conscious choice because we're observing what's going on without judging. Paying attention to events *in the moment* is the technique you need to learn to help you to pause when you need to. Viktor Frankl, an Austrian neurologist, psychologist and Holocaust survivor, is commonly attributed with neatly summing up the importance of that pause when he said:

> 'Between stimulus and response there is a space. In that space is our power to choose our response. In our response lies our growth and freedom.'

Successive studies have shown that widespread adoption of mindful practices can improve employee performance, mental health and resilience. A twelve-month study by the UK government's Mindfulness All Party Parliamentary Group found a 33% reduction in stress for those doing mindfulness training, with 92% reporting improvements in the way they managed strong feelings and emotions.[4] Daniel Goleman and University of Wisconsin-Madison neuroscientist Richard Davidson identified three proven benefits of mindfulness in their book *Altered Traits*.[5] It promotes focus and a clarity of thought, a sense of calm open-mindedness and improved cognitive ability.

Hardly surprisingly, the corporate world has begun to sit up to take notice. Attending mindfulness classes has become a popular way to begin the workday at many large organisations, particularly within tech firms such as Apple, Facebook, LinkedIn and Twitter. That reach is extending, though. While one might not immediately imagine an engineering organisation at the forefront of progressive thinking as far as employee relations goes, international company Bosch could prove you wrong. Bosch uses mindfulness to train 1,000 executives in its leadership programmes, citing it as an essential mechanism to shift away from a culture of control to one of trust.[6]

US health insurer Aetna has taken this one step further, training 13,000 employees in mindfulness. Aside from the benefits for each individual, this is paying dividends for the organisation, which reports a reduction in stress levels of 28% and an estimated $3,000 per employee in annual productivity improvements.

Even if there is currently no formal mindfulness process available to you, start practising it today. Learning how to pause doesn't require forty-five minutes in a darkened room (I wouldn't discourage this, but few people, including me, have the time or patience for this sort of activity). You can achieve amazing results by practising acts of mindfulness for a few minutes at a time over the course of a day.

> **Hajar El Haddaoui, Senior Director and Executive Board Member, NTT Limited**
>
> I have slots in my agenda which are called oxygen time. This where I catch up with people that I didn't have time for such as colleagues, family and friends. After work, I take some time. I go outside, take in some oxygen and reflect. This gives me a sense of living and purpose besides my work and career.
>
> For me, there is no professional life and private life. There is just life and we need to be connected to ourselves and enjoy it fully.

When you take a shower first thing in the morning, instead of thinking about what you're doing for the rest of the day, be in the moment. Enjoy the sensation of the water running over your body and the scent of your favourite soap and nothing else.

Alternatively, have a mindful walk to work. Take a moment to look at the trees and to notice the seasonal changes and the sun on your face. As the day progresses, build in a break for a mindful coffee at eleven o'clock and really taste that coffee, rather than gulping it down ahead of the next meeting. Make the conscious decision to look out of the window at least once a day.

I live in a beautiful region, close to a lake with mountains behind it. Even though I've been there more than twenty years, it makes me feel so happy when I glimpse the beautiful view. It doesn't take long, perhaps only sixty seconds, but I know it will change the next few hours for me.

If you are not feeling confident to begin with, there are a number of apps to help you get into mindfulness practice such as Headspace, Calm and Balance Meditation. Download one to your phone and it will take you through a series of exercises which will train you to be more mindful. Research from one app shows that within just ten days, users will experience a 14% decrease in stress and a 27% decrease in irritability.[7] After three weeks of mindfulness practice, users were 57% less aggressive and reactive towards negative feedback and 23% demonstrated more compassionate behaviour.

Once you get into the habit, each of these mindful experiences only needs take a few moments out of your day, but the more you do it, the more you will be able to assess yourself and how you're doing. Mindfulness helps you be in the present and become more aware of what's going on. It creates a period where you are not distracted by all the thoughts about the day ahead that would normally crowd your brain.

Tool #2 – Take an inventory of your emotions

Take a look at the emotion and energy management grid below. In the context of your previous day at work, which square on the grid would you say best describes the emotions that dominated your day? Were you mostly frustrated and annoyed? Did you pass the day in a state of calm contentment, grateful to be doing your job?

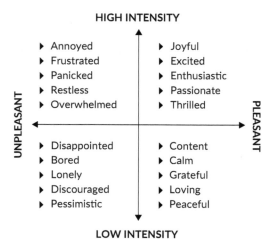

Emotion and energy management

In an ideal world, you would spend the majority of your working days experiencing the emotions listed on the right-hand side of the grid. Both top and bottom squares list pleasant, nourishing emotions, with the ones on the top right being high impact. The ones on the bottom right are more low impact, energy giving and karmic.

While it might sound nice and motivating to live life at a million miles an hour, experiencing the high-impact emotion of continual passion and excitement in the top right square, you do need to recharge and rebalance at times. Hence you need to spend some time in the low-intensity corner on the bottom right of the grid. This is the recharge and renewal zone that will give you time to reflect, gain some perspective and be an effective leader.

The opposite side of the grid features energy-draining emotions. The high-impact corner at the top-left side of the grid is reserved for strong emotions such as fear and anxiety that drain all our energy. This square is the survival zone. While our emotions are high intensity and powerful, they are not coming from a good place.

In a typical scenario, you may find yourself running around trying to meet the demands of numerous people while simultaneously juggling other pressures in your life. Of course, you can perform in this zone for a while, but if you push it too hard for too long, you might then enter the bottom left of this grid, which is the burnout zone. Here you will find yourself feeling tired and even depressed. After an intense period of depleting your stocks of energy, you have reached the stage of running on empty. If you and your team find yourself in constant survival mode, you need to be aware of it so you can implement the tools and strategies to recharge, bring yourselves back up and move over to the right-hand side of this grid.

At this learning stage, as you gradually develop awareness of your emotions, it's useful to regularly repeat the exercise of evaluating where you are on the grid. At the end of every working day, stop and take an analysis. Where did you see yourself on the grid that day? Were you mostly at the top or bottom of the left or right side?

You may find yourself at different places on the grid each day, but a pattern will emerge. Doing this exercise will help you evaluate your current situation so you can move on to strategies to manage your position on the grid and ensure a balance between high and low intensity emotions.

Tool #3 – Emotions are meant to be felt

One of the lessons you may have picked up from Tool #2 is that it can be challenging to articulate your emotions at the end of the day. You might perhaps realise that you didn't have the best of days, but can't quite place your predominant emotions.

If this is the case for you, you are not alone. Most people don't allow themselves time to properly assess their feelings. This is a skill that I have had to develop as I live a lot of my life in my head – or am very 'cerebral', as others have put it. If you are like me, you will often be disconnected with your body and not even notice the physical sensations that it is experiencing.

We all feel emotions in a different way. When I'm angry, I feel a tightening in my throat. Some people might experience a pressure at the base of their neck or a sense of heat rising in their face. When I am sad, I feel a knot in my stomach. Others become lethargic or lose their appetite.

When I ask you to tell me the physical symptoms of anger or sadness and how they impact you, you may be able to answer the question straight away. If, however, you find it difficult, there is a useful exercise you can do. It's a quick scan for noticing emotions and only needs to take a couple of minutes.

Close your eyes and take a few deep breaths. Notice how your feet touch the floor and your arms, legs and back feel as they come into contact with your chair. Pay attention to your breaths and how your chest rises and falls as you breathe.

Now, think back to a recent time when you experienced an unpleasant emotion such as anger. Relive that emotion in your mind and take a moment to notice where you're feeling it. Is it in your chest, in your stomach or in another part of your body? Allow yourself to magnify that feeling to the point where it might feel quite unpleasant. Memorise that sensation, and then switch your thoughts to something nice and dwell on it for a while so the unpleasant feelings completely disappear.

While this exercise is not pleasant to do, it will help you tune into how you experience different emotions. Try it for other energy-draining emotions such as fear or sadness. Over time, when you do the daily emotion and energy management grid review detailed in Tool #2, you will find it easier to note your predominant emotions.

Tool #4 – Identify/label

How often do you simply say 'I'm fine' when asked how you are, even when this is far from the case? It's become a reflex response for most of us, so it's rare for anyone to say when they are not 100%. In reply, your interlocutor says, 'That's great' and everyone goes on their way.

In the workplace, 'I'm fine' is usually deemed to be the most appropriate response, and in most cases it is. A passing greeting in the corridor is not the time or place to bare our souls, but there are times when we do need to be more adept at articulating our feelings, even if only to ourselves.

As per the previous two tools, the goal here is to become more familiar with how we are feeling. Once we label our emotions, we're paying attention to them. When we pay attention, then we can start to understand how we are feeling and become better equipped at reducing the impact of certain emotions. Labelling an emotion makes it into a concrete concept rather than just a thing that's happening to us.

STUDY: Feelings into words[8]

In 2012, a group of researchers at UCLA in the US carried out an experiment based on people's fear of spiders. They wanted to see if labelling our emotions significantly reduces the stress.

A group of people were asked to go outside and were shown a box which, they were informed, contained a large, hairy spider. They were invited to walk towards the box, open it and reach inside to touch the spider.

When the participants were brought back inside, they were split into four groups. The first group was asked to articulate how they had felt. The reaction was, hardly surprisingly, something along the lines of: 'I am frightened of that big, hairy tarantula.' The second group was encouraged to downplay their fears. They were invited to reassure themselves by saying something like, 'It's a spider in a box. It can't hurt me. I don't need to be afraid.' The third group was asked to say something completely irrelevant, commenting on, say, the weather that day. Meanwhile, the fourth group was not asked to say anything. Then, the participants were invited to go outside again and repeat the exercise. Could they, the researchers asked, walk towards the box, reach inside and touch the spider?

What were the results? The first group, who had been asked to label their fears, far outperformed all the other groups. Their palms were much less sweaty and they got much closer to the tarantula. They had named their fears and, as a result, were better equipped to embrace them.

In the same way as we often struggle to articulate our feelings, we also find it tough to label emotions. This is partly because we don't tend to talk about them, other than the ubiquitous 'I'm fine'. However, another part of the problem is there are a huge number of different emotions to choose from. While most of us can name a handful of the main ones such as fear, anger, sadness and happiness, we usually dry up after that.

In the following table, I have shared a list of different emotions. Many of them are nuanced from some of the main ones you are familiar with. Now, when you're checking through your emotions, think about this list and use it to help you properly understand what you're feeling. Are you angry with your colleague or simply frustrated? Are you sad or actually bored?

Afraid	**Connected**	**Angry**	**Centred**	**Ashamed**
Panicked	Affectionate	Furious	Relieved	Guilty
Overwhelmed	Compassionate	Annoyed	Hopeful	Embarrassed
Restless	Loving	Jealous	Serene	Insignificant
Anxious	Sensual	Helpless	Secure	Humiliated
Confused	Caring	Enraged	Free	Awkward
Frantic	Grateful	Frustrated	Calm	Insecure
Nervous	Passionate	Impatient	Clear	Worthless
Worried	Loved	Irritable	Peaceful	
Hesitant	Accepted	Resentful	Whole	
Terrified				

Proud	**Sad**	**Happy**	**Awed**	**Disgusted**
Confident	Grief	Alive	Curious	Shocked
Capable	Lonely	Excited	Moved	Hateful
Determined	Disappointed	Joyful	Inspired	Dislike
Strong	Hopeless	Carefree	Impressed	
Fulfilled	Depressed	Ecstatic	Engaged	
Brave	Miserable	Motivated		
Appreciated	Empty	Delighted		
Honoured	Lost	Playful		
Respected	Regretful			
	Disconnected			
	Bored			

Emotion checklist

As with all the tools here, it will take some practice to identify and articulate your true emotions. You might like to enlist your family or close friends to help. Explain that you want to get more in tune with your emotions and would like to do a regular exercise to properly describe how you've been feeling that day. Invite them to tell you how they are feeling too, using words from the list above. If, say, someone tells you that an event made them sad, challenge them to be more precise.

Ask, 'Are there any other emotions on this list that sum up your feelings more accurately?'

The more you practise, the more you'll become familiar with the different emotions. Once you've become adept at identifying your emotions, the next step is to understand what's behind each one, so the more precise you are with articulating your feelings, the easier it's going to be to understand them.

Tool #5 – Understanding

Understanding emotions begins when you answer the question why. '*Why* do I feel this way?' The goal here is to get a handle on the underlying reason for the feelings you have been so carefully detecting and articulating using the tools in the previous sections. It is where you analyse what it is that is *causing* you to feel this way and what's behind the message of the emotion.

When we feel any emotion, it is rarely straight-forward. There may be a complex web of events and memories leading up to this moment, where one emotion will lead on to or provoke another. A bit of probing may be required to get to the bottom of what is going on.

Be prepared, though: if you ask yourself one question about how you are feeling, it often leads on to more questions. It's helpful to have some pre-prepared questions that you can use to help you be that emotional detective I mentioned earlier and dig deep to get to the real reason for how you feel.

Your questions could include:

- What has just happened?

- What physical sensations am I feeling?

- What could have caused this feeling?

- What happened earlier today or yesterday?

- What else is going on here?

- Why now?

Sometimes, your initial assumptions about the way you are feeling can be wrong. Say, for example, you are in a meeting and your boss singles you out for criticism. It will inevitably be a tense moment, particularly if voices are raised.

Your first reaction might be to feel shame or embarrassment because this is happening in front of the whole team, but there could be many underlying emotions adding to your discomfort. You may be anxious because you know that you have made a mistake or haven't carried out your job as well as you should. Perhaps this is not the first time this has happened and you may privately fear you could be fired, yet the reason you have been distracted of late is you don't find your job terribly stretching, so you are bored and frustrated too.

In a situation like this, it is crucial to analyse all the underlying themes that have led up to this moment. Understanding what is really going on will take a bit of time, which is why that mindful moment of pause is so useful. Once you have clarity, you will be better equipped to work out what to do next. In the case here, for example, rather than feeling crushed by the admonishment, your time might be better spent requesting a one-to-one with the team leader to have an honest discussion about your career.

Tool #6 – Regulation

By this stage, you will be aware that we are all constantly flooded with a stream of emotions. With so much going on, it is clear we need to regulate at least some of them or we'd be all over the place. It is not, however, a given that we endeavour to halt any energy-sapping emotions and only give free rein to the 'good' emotions. Each emotion has a time and a place and, at some point, may be crucial in helping us achieve our goals.

Take, as an example, anger, which is firmly in the high-impact energy-draining list. Anger can be highly effective in some circumstances, such as when you need to present a powerful argument or fight for permission or staunchly defend a position. In these circumstances, you shouldn't attempt to dampen a short blast of passionate anger.

Of course, at other times, anger is not useful at all and will need to be toned down. If you learn to recognise emotions, it is much easier to decide when to dial them up or down. That's what the regulation is.

The actual process of regulating our emotions is nothing new. In fact, everyone instinctively does it from shortly after the time we were born. When you see a baby sucking their thumb, that is a classic example of emotional regulation. The infant is comforting him or herself because they feel a bit distressed or tired.

As we grow older and life becomes more complex, our response is less instinctive and we need to learn strategies to regulate the flood of emotions we encounter. These strategies will fall into two distinct groups: regulating in the moment and regulating long term. Let's take a look at each one.

Short-term regulation strategies

These strategies are there to help you in the moment when an event sets off a strong emotional response. It might be that a meeting is suddenly cancelled, throwing your plans into chaos, or perhaps a colleague or senior executive says something that provokes a range of energy-sapping emotions. By this stage, you will have done enough work to recognise the impact and pay attention to your feelings about what is happening. While there may not always be time to fully understand the intense emotion that results, you know you must do something.

One of the most useful ways to regulate your response is to use the STOP technique, a four-step mental checklist that will help you pause and respond more appropriately.[9] As soon as you detect an intense emotional response:

- **S**top what you're doing, even if only for a few seconds.

- **T**ake a few deep breaths to bring yourself into the present moment. Breathing helps you connect with your body.

- **O**bserve what's going on. This gives you the space to quickly decide how to react. If, say, someone is criticising you, you might excuse yourself, saying you are going to get a glass of water.

- **P**roceed. You've made the decision, now follow through and do it.

Another useful short-term regulation technique is anchoring. In a situation such as a meeting where somebody says or does something that makes you unhappy, physically anchor yourself. This might mean touching the table in front of you or placing your feet more firmly on the floor or focusing on your breathing. Each one of these conscious movements will bring you back into the present moment and give you space to make an informed choice about how to react.

Long-term regulation

These strategies are useful for the emotions you know you are going to encounter day after day. Long-term regulation borrows strongly from the Danish concept of *hygge*, which is learning how to find comfort and pleasure in simple, soothing moments. Think of long-term regulation as like an emotional hygge. You're setting yourself up for recurring emotions, and then relaxing after. Maintain mindful breaks throughout the day, and then make room for regular pleasurable pauses.

It might help to imagine yourself as an emotional sponge, swelling up as the day goes along with all the accumulated emotions you experience. Your emotional hygge is a way of squeezing out all the emotions at the end of the day.

How you do it is up to you. Everybody is different, so you will need to decide what is the best technique for you. For some people, it is having a shower. Others might prefer sport or doing something creative. Others still might prefer talking, venting or hugging people. Alternatively, there are breathing exercises or meditation techniques. Whatever it is, make it something you like doing.

The goal is that when you go to bed, you've worked with your emotions. There's nothing worse than coming home from an emotional day and just ignoring it.

What happens when we don't deal with difficult emotions? Generally, we will either brood or bottle, neither of which is healthy. Brooding is where we become so consumed with something that we can't think about anything else. It goes round and round our brain as we ruminate over it and think about it from every angle: *She must have known that her criticism would upset me. But could I have done it differently? Why did she word it like that?* Left undealt with, it can become a bit of an obsession.

Bottling, on the other hand, is where we push the emotions away and try not to think about them. Perhaps we feel exploited or betrayed, but decide it is better to lock away – or bottle – any thoughts of hurt or resentment and not even acknowledge them.

Neither bottling nor brooding is good for our mental health. Over time, either can lead to low levels of happiness and raised levels of sadness and anxiety.

Eventually, you might like to extend your long-term regulation practice to include some trigger work. We all have triggers. These are events that make us blow up disproportionately and react in a way that is out of kilter with the event that caused it. These triggers are personal, often linked to something in our past, perhaps a wound from a painful situation or a feeling of being inadequate. Unfortunately, there are always people who seem to know exactly how to press that trigger, and then sit back to enjoy watching us go completely ballistic.

The first step here is to become an emotional detective and notice your triggers. When is it that you get ridiculously angry or become overly fearful? Get in touch with when and why that happens. You might like to keep a journal for two or perhaps three weeks. Divide each page into four: events, emotion, thoughts and behaviour. Each day, record something that happened and your emotional response to it. What did you think? How did you behave?

This journal will help you build awareness of your triggers and situations you always find uncomfortable. Now deploy your emotional hygge to anticipate these events and build in time around them to unwind and regulate your emotions.

Techniques like this are not *always* going to work. We are all only human and we will sometimes get overwhelmed by a strong emotion, but if we have adopted the habit of being mindful throughout the day and taking regular breaks, this is where the long-term regulation comes in as we'll be more likely to be able to control our response.

Tool #7 – Reappraisal

Sometimes noticing your triggers is not enough, however well-practised your emotional hygge. Hence the need for the final tool in this section, reappraisal. Reappraisal is the ability to step back from a situation and see it from a different perspective, in a similar way to James Gross's techniques outlined at the start of the chapter.

To understand how reappraisal might work, consider this scenario. You are working from home, doing your utmost to complete a complex piece of work that has to be finished before the end of the day, and your four-year-old is seriously acting up. You've tried all the usual tricks and bribes and nothing is working. With the clock ticking towards your deadline, you are at your wits' end. You are seconds away from shouting at your child and quite possibly overreacting.

What if you could pause for a moment and reframe the situation? During that pause, you would realise this youngster has been stuck indoors all day and didn't really get out much the day before. In fact, their acting up is them simply letting off a little steam, which is quite healthy.

Once you reappraise the situation, you can think more rationally. It won't be the end of the world for the piece of work to be sent at 9pm rather than 6pm. After all, no one will look at it until at least tomorrow anyhow. If you give your child some attention now, you could always catch up later this evening when they are in bed. Suddenly, your reaction to the interruption is completely different to how it might have been.

We all have our own perspective of events, but we can train ourselves to see another point of view. This is well illustrated by the following picture, known as the Young woman, old woman, which was created by an anonymous illustrator in late nineteenth-century Germany.

Young woman, old woman

What do you see? A young or an old woman? If you see a young woman, train your gaze on her chin and think of it as a large nose. Look also at the ear and think of it as an eye. If, on the other hand, you see the old woman, look at her nose and think of it as the left cheek of a face looking away from you. Reconsider her eye as an ear and the young lady is revealed.

Reappraisal is a skill that takes a lot of work to learn, but if you find yourself being triggered by something regularly, it is worth spending some time on it. The likelihood then is that when you consider what has really created such a strong emotional reaction, you will see it differently. It is quite likely that the next time it happens, you won't get triggered so much. You may even eventually stop getting triggered at all by this event.

While emotions play a crucial role in your working life, they can intensify to a point where they feel out of control. With a little practice, you can take back the reins and work with your emotions, rather than repress, bottle or brood over them. It begins with identifying what you are feeling, accepting *all* your emotions, and then using techniques to regulate and occasionally reappraise them.

Often, this will require hitting the pause button to give yourself some distance from intense emotions, so you can work out a more reasonable way to react. You may even need to physically distance yourself from a trigger. Over time and with practice and mindfulness, you will increase your awareness of feelings and experiences and use your emotions more productively.

Summary

It is essential that we welcome *all* emotions, pleasant and unpleasant, accepting them as they arise. This chapter has set out how this acceptance can unfold and the tools that we can use to work with our emotions more effectively. These tools all take practice; they're not an instant solution, but over time, they will allow us to recognise and regulate our emotions.

FOUR
Managing Fear Of Change

There is so much uncertainty in the world. Human beings are hard-wired to fear change, yet we face new challenges on all sides. At the time of writing, we are experiencing an extensive economic downturn with a corresponding severe impact on our cost of living. Countries the world over are riven by political division and even war, which is in turn adding to the economic uncertainty and heightening fears over future food shortages thanks to supply-chain issues. All of this comes at a time when so many of us believe we should be focusing our energies on working together to find solutions to the now-pressing environmental crisis.

There are multiple challenges in the workplace too, each one involving change to a greater or lesser extent. Some of the most significant are concerns about job security as developments in technology make many roles redundant. Likewise, the likelihood of organisational change, which often increases during economic downturns, such as mergers, takeovers or corporate restructuring will inevitably have an impact on everyone in employment.

On a smaller scale, we might experience a change to our work equipment or the workplaces where we operate out of day to day. There may be a reshuffle of teams, which may or may not coincide with a new team leader. Meanwhile, everyone is under pressure to do more, produce more and be the best. It's no wonder so many of us are buckling under the strain.

Whatever the change, however large or small, the one thing we can be certain of is that emotions will be involved. Our brains don't like change or any sort of ambiguity or uncertainty. We prefer to predict and make sense of the world and are comfortable and feel safe when things appear stable and as expected. The stress and fear that we highlighted in the piece on learning in Chapter Two are increased during times of uncertainty. When a change comes our way, we not only have an emotional rection but also have a mindset; a belief about what this may mean to us. These beliefs are the result of our life history, previous experiences and personality predispositions. In other words, we interpret change based on all of this.

Our beliefs can at times be limiting and can make us negative or prevent us from moving forward. If we can identify these beliefs and work with them, challenging them for example, when necessary, then we can increase our positivity and this is important work that sits alongside the emotional work we must do during change.

For those who can find the positive in change, they may feel hope, enjoy the anticipation of a new direction and have faith that it will create something better in the future. They may even throw themselves full-heartedly into the change and participate in its implementation.

There are others who find change extremely uncomfortable. In fact, I'd say they are in the majority. These people may deny the reality of the change altogether, burying their heads in the sand and displaying emotions such as resentment, frustration and anger. In these situations, unless they understand and work with these emotions, it can negatively impact the individuals' health and wellbeing at work.

Dealing with the fear of change

When we are individuals facing change, whether in our personal or professional lives, there are some strategies that we can adopt to make things easier. Key to this is to learn to acknowledge and even welcome fear into our lives. We need to accept that we cannot overcome or beat fear or, worse still, ignore it altogether.

In my business, I have seen many clients struggle with their mental health during challenging times at work. Their fears stem from a variety of reasons. The most common one is that the individual concerned becomes convinced they will lose their job, but there are many other triggers too, nearly all centring around a potential change, whether real or imagined. In each case, it is only by learning how to work with their fears that they can manage the impending change effectively.

Let me give you the example of one senior executive who I will call Bob here. At the start of the pandemic, Bob was in charge of a team of thirty people. Like so many others, he soon found himself managing a remote team for the first time, trying to engage and motivate people who were themselves worried about their own situations. Bob's already challenging task was compounded by two further factors, one at work and one at home.

There was a real possibility of redundancies in Bob's department as his firm struggled to keep its order book stable in the changed circumstances. Meanwhile, Bob's wife was pregnant and in the high-risk category for COVID-19.

Up until this point, Bob had been doing well. At least, that was the impression from the outside, but now the cracks were starting to show. Bob was getting into conflicts with his colleagues on a regular basis. When he wasn't snapping at his co-workers, he was quiet and withdrawn. While he had previously been a high achiever, his work was suffering. He was missing deadlines and making mistakes.

When I began working with Bob, he was close to burnout and on sick leave. It was immediately obvious that he found the idea of talking about his own emotions hard and when it came to articulating his fears, that was something he found well-nigh impossible. Bob was a smart man and a tough leader who had been raised to keep pushing forward and not dwell on his emotions. At first, the most he would concede was that he was feeling a little isolated and had been having trouble sleeping. Under encouragement, he did admit he was concerned this might impact his long-term health.

As Bob and I continued to work together, we discovered that his ill health, emotional outbursts and changes in behaviour at work all stemmed from a long-term pattern of suppressing his emotions and ignoring his fears. During our coaching sessions, Bob was able to get in touch with his greatest fears and understand what was behind them. Just by welcoming them and being with them over a few minutes, he found the fear subsiding.

Over time and by regularly repeating this process, Bob observed a drop in his anxiety levels. Under my encouragement, he started writing a journal, recording the triggers that provoked his anxiety. He also talked about them with his friends and colleagues. By becoming more willing to explore his fears, Bob found a way to work with them rather than be controlled by them.

As someone who has over a long period of time struggled with fear and anxiety, I have always been interested in the background to the emotion. The part of our brain that is sometimes referred to as the 'reptilian brain', which has been responsible for our survival for millions of years, sends out messages of fear, ensuring we are always on the lookout for anything that might hurt us. The reptilian brain is really persistent, sending us into fight, flight or freeze in response to the slightest concern, even when there may not be any actual danger.

When we are at work, we are prompted into a fear response by change or challenge. We also suffer from enduring underlying fears such as not being good enough, being rejected by our colleagues or customers, or failing. If we are accustomed to seeing fear as negative and try to push it away, or attempt to mask or dampen it by taking medication, it will always resurface anyhow. Even when we use logic, addressing our fears in a rational way by using the thinking part of the brain to reason them out to their logical conclusion and therefore debunk them, this will not deal with the fear in the long term.

There is, however, an approach that does work. Bear with me on this one: it may well go contrary to your instincts because it concerns the feelings that fear produces. We all hate the physical symptoms of fear such as sweaty palms or a tightening in the chest, but what I encourage people to do is to *move towards* the fear and to feel it in their bodies. You need to acknowledge and accept it and, most importantly, listen to the message that the fear is there to convey. As I've previously highlighted, you need to understand the purpose of this emotion.

Embracing fear may not come naturally to you. It doesn't with many people. What has done the trick for me has been to start by acknowledging the fear, sitting with it for a minute or two and even thanking it for being present. After all, it is there for a purpose.

Sitting with this emotion and doing the emotional work outlined in the previous chapter is the first step to working with fear rather than pushing it away. It can be useful to acknowledge in that moment that you may not have the answers but, while the feeling is unpleasant, it will also not last long. For a hyper achiever like me who constantly measures themselves on their results, this can be hard to do, but I do feel the pressure release and the anxiety quickly diminishes.

When you do this exercise, you will see that emotions pass. Even if the fear returns at a later stage, this practice of welcoming and accepting it is invaluable when you are faced with uncertainty or change.

The change curve

During our leadership training, my team and I give leaders a tool which we call the change curve, developed by Elisabeth Kübler-Ross. You can read more about it at the following website: www.cleverism. com/understanding-kubler-ross-change-curve. You may be familiar with the grief curve, which follows the five stages of grief from denial to anger, bargaining, depression and acceptance. This curve follows the same principle, plotting the path through the emotional rollercoaster that people experience during the process of change. In this instance the stages are shock, denial, frustration, depression, experiment, decision and finally integration.

When I work with individuals using this curve, I invite them to say where they currently see themselves. At what stage is their emotional response?

What are the emotions they are experiencing? This exercise helps them to recognise their emotional journey and to better understand that this is a normal process for everyone.

It is interesting to note that throughout the change process, we can all experience conflicting emotions at the same time. We can, for example, be sad about what we are losing and joyful about the prospect of a better future.

Those in a position of leadership can make good use of this curve at times when significant change is underway by sharing it with their team to help them better understand their own emotions. Leaders need to realise that we don't all travel along the curve at the same speed. Some individuals will need more support than others at different stages.

Frederic Van Mullem, Vice President Human Resources, Medtronic

I recently experienced a situation where a reorganisation of my company had been announced which resulted in my position being eliminated. The announcement came quickly, which obviously generated a lot of anxiety in my team and triggered much questioning and fear. Some people said they felt quite numb and fatigued.

I acknowledged my concerns, yet did not want to position myself as a victim. Rather, I wanted to help the team and organisation transition to a new phase as well as point out that these situations come with a range of opportunities that we may not see upfront.

> When I met with my team again, after having given them the chance to digest my point of view, I gave them the opportunity to vent. They needed to express their frustration and fears.

Take, as an example, a time of organisational change. The process of change is fundamentally about feelings. The starting point to helping teams accept and even welcome that change, as well as fully contribute to it, is for those in charge of implementing it to accept that emotions are an essential part of the mix and to work through the implications of the changes on the curve.

Ignoring the emotional factor could well impair the chances of successful implementation on many levels. There may be a detrimental impact on an individual team member's health and wellbeing, which will also influence their performance. When we don't like change and believe it could be potentially damaging to us, we tend to resist it as much as possible.

By understanding the change curve, team leaders will be aware that there may be a drop in productivity and performance when a change is announced. This is the time when individuals are shocked at the news and go into their natural fight, flight or fright mode as they worry about the unknown. If a team member is at the denial stage, looking for evidence the change is not really happening, managers can help by providing as much information to them as possible. Communication is key, as is providing a safe space for the team members to voice their concerns.

In the next stage, where individuals become angry or frustrated, there may well be some blaming or finger-pointing in the team as the reality sinks in and emotions surface. When this anger subsides into sadness, leaders and team members need to acknowledge what is being lost. Sadness is a very important stage in accepting change and needs to happen before anyone can move back up the curve. Leaders must continue listening to the views of their teams, reassuring them and giving them what they need so they can move on with confidence. As employees head back up the curve, coming to terms with the change, they will still need support as their moods will continue to fluctuate until everything has been fully integrated.

The emotional culture of an organisation and the way in which emotions are encouraged to be expressed or suppressed will play a great role in the success of any change programme. Emotionally intelligent managers act to reduce stress and anxiety in their team by reading the emotions of others and understanding where they are on the change curve. They can then take actions to manage those emotions before problems arise.

This helps individuals on the team to make sense of their own and others' emotions during times of upheaval. They are then better equipped to positively contribute to the process of change and influence the response of others so everyone contributes. As a result, everyone will be more resilient and better able to regulate their stress levels.

When change is performed *with* people rather than foisted upon them, the anxiety and fear around the process can be reduced. Everyone should be consulted and included and the process entirely transparent. This means team leaders must not only explain the changes, but also actively listen to the hopes, fears and needs of the individuals going through the change. This is the crucial first step in breaking down any resistance they may encounter.

Summary

In this chapter, we have looked at an emotion we're all likely to feel from time to time: fear, and in particular, fear of change. Whatever the change, however large or small, the one thing we can be certain of is that emotions will be involved.

There are those who can find the positive in change, enjoying the anticipation of a new direction and having faith it will create something better in the future. There are others who find change extremely uncomfortable. These people may deny the reality of the change altogether. Unless they understand and work with these emotions, it can negatively impact these individuals' health and wellbeing at work. Leaders can have a key role in helping their team members during change by providing a space for emotion and encouraging them to connect to how they are feeling.

PART TWO
THE EMOTIONALLY INTELLIGENT LEADER

FIVE
Leading With Emotion

It's a cliché to say employees don't leave bad jobs, they leave bad bosses, but like all such sayings, there is a ring of truth to it and never more so than today. One of the clear trends of the Great Resignation is employees are leaving businesses (and business leaders) that don't care to join ones that do.

To win the escalating war for talent, business leaders need emotional skills. More specifically, emotional leadership is what will make all the difference in employees finding the trust and connection that we all crave today.

STUDY: What management style creates the highest level of employee satisfaction?[1]

Traditional thinking has it that leaders need to be tough to get the most out of their employees.WAfter all, successful leaders must hold their teams fully accountable, set high standards, push for stringent monitoring of any failures as well as successes and, often, make painful decisions.

In this study, leadership experts Jack Zenger and Joseph Folkman wanted to know: is tough enough? Would employees prefer their leaders to be kinder and more empathetic? A survey of 161,000 employees working for 31,000 leaders rooted out those who expressed the greatest levels of satisfaction. Focusing on these employees, Zenger and Folkman found:

- 8.9% of those who had *tough* leaders were in the top 10% of satisfied employees
- 6.7% of those who had *nice* leaders were in the top 10%
- 68% of those who had both *tough* and *nice* leaders were in the top 10%

In leadership, toughness is not enough. To be a good leader today and fully engage the humanforce, we need to match this skill by connecting with the team on an *emotional* level. Creating a human connection is the way to demonstrate that people are an asset, not just a resource.

The importance of connecting on an emotional level was, like so many things, amplified by the pandemic. Who among us wasn't alarmed and unsure what to do when the crisis hit almost overnight? The circumstance brought out the best in some leaders – both political and corporate – and the worst in others.

Those leaders who demonstrated a high degree of EQ were frequently viewed more favourably than those who wanted to tough it out or ignore fears about COVID-19, often trying to usher things back to business-as-usual long before the all-clear was sounded. Emotionally aware leaders were responsive to how others were feeling, were prepared to work with those emotions and demonstrated assertiveness and flexibility.

While the pandemic was, we hope, a once-in-a-lifetime event, we are still facing substantial changes on all fronts, as already documented in this book. Some challenges are a direct result of the fallout from the health crisis, others came about because of changes in the workplace that were already in train. The pace of work is getting faster and faster, which is a challenge we need to navigate against all the new skills we require in technology and adapting to new working practices.

Meanwhile, there is huge uncertainty about which jobs will still exist in the future. One study shows 44% of occupations are declining.[2] An analysis of 366 occupations shows employment levels dropping in 160 of them. At the time of the report, these occupations employed around 10 million people in the UK, down from 13.2 million in a decade and a half. The most in-demand skills for employers today are oral comprehension and expression, active listening and speaking.

Emotional intelligence

In this rapidly changing world, leaders at all levels need EQ to help their teams navigate all this stress and uncertainty. Just ignoring any anxiety and expecting everyone to get on with delivering the results is not going to work. Leaders need people skills to work effectively with their teams.

Take, as an example, the trend towards hybrid working. Those employees in favour of the more flexible model speak glowingly about improved well-being, the boost to their work-life balance and income thanks to less commuting and, of course, the pleasure of spending more time with loved ones. In fact, half of those workers with access to hybrid working would resign if this option were removed.[3] Those employers that are supportive of the hybrid model report improved productivity, engagement and job retention.

The big question here is how do organisations retain and reinforce the emotional connection with remote workers? Even employees who welcome homeworking admit to occasionally feeling lonely and disconnected, particularly those in single-person households who can spend every waking hour on their own. There's a huge need for companies to invest in connection building and that involves a lot of EQ work.

Success in managing an emotionally intelligent workplace is down to emotionally intelligent leaders. Leaders with a high EQ understand their people well, can perceive what they are feeling and act upon it. This helps teams on multiple fronts. It:

- **Builds trust.** Emotionally intelligent leaders come across as authentic because they use their emotions in a genuine way, which encourages employees to trust them.

- **Reduces fear of failure.** Employees treated with compassion are more likely to forgive mistakes and have less fear of failure and more resilience when things do go wrong than those who aren't. They are also more likely to act compassionately towards others.

- **Has a positive health impact.** Employees with empathetic managers have been shown to have lower levels of psychosomatic complaints or physical symptoms like headaches, high blood pressure and stomach aches than those whose leaders don't prioritise EQ.[4]

It's impossible to be a successful leader today without EQ. It might be possible to wing it for a while, but ultimately, there will be challenges in the workplace that can't be overcome by telling everyone to get on with it (if, indeed, that ever worked). Any leader who does not have EQ is going to struggle to overcome those challenges.

STUDY: Emotional competence and leadership excellence at Johnson & Johnson[5]

To explore whether there are specific leadership skills that distinguish high performers from low performers, consumer and healthcare group Johnson & Johnson surveyed 358 managers from around the globe, as well as 1,400 employees. The highest-performing managers were rated to have significantly more emotional competence than their lower-performing counterparts.

Those who received the highest ratings scored most highly across all four of the EQ categories listed in the poll: self-awareness, self-management, social awareness and social skills. The organisation subsequently modified its Standards of Leadership model to include provision for selection, assessment and development in emotional skills. Educational programmes were also developed and launched across the business to familiarise all employees with the concept of emotional, social and relational competency.

Do you lead with EQ?

My work at HumanForce centres around encouraging teams to connect at an emotional level with their colleagues. A question I often ask the executives I coach is: 'What's your approach to balancing your goals with the need to be *interested* in your people?' While the majority seem to recognise they do indeed need to do this, the reaction I often get is that they simply don't have the time.

'I know I *should* be talking more with my team, but I'm just so busy running around trying to get everything done,' is a common response. My counter argument is that building relationships like this is an important use of their time.

Occasionally, there is a mismatch between how leaders rate their levels of EQ and how others perceive them. In almost all cases, the mismatch comes about because leaders err on the over-optimistic side, believing they have a very high EQ indeed, thank you very much, and use it to full effect at work. This belief is not always completely borne out by the result of the 2.0 EQ test we use at HumanForce. This includes 360-degree feedback across the board from peers, direct reports and managers, who don't all tend to agree with this confident assessment.

As a rule of thumb, it's those who do, in fact, have a low EQ that tend towards substantially overrating their skills in this department. Those with a high EQ are usually fairly in tune with the extent of their abilities to connect with the team. However, even with those who are in tune with their strengths in this department, there's usually evidence of blind spots and areas where they could do better.

There are leaders who simply don't recognise the need for a high EQ at all or at least don't regard it as a priority. This was the case for someone – let's call him Julian – who was managing a large team in a technical environment. He was a nice guy, yet constantly in conflict with his team.

I was called in by his firm's HR department to get to the bottom of what was happening and resolve the never-ending conflicts within Julian's team. When Julian and I first spoke, it was clear that he had high expectations of himself and equally high expectations of the team. Performance was everything to him.

The trouble was that this goal was to the exclusion of all other considerations. He barely if ever spoke to his colleagues in an informal way. He wouldn't ask them how they were or about their weekends or holidays. He definitely didn't have a clue about the dates of all their birthdays. Each day, he'd simply pass on instructions, and then return where necessary to check in on the work they were doing. When I asked him about this, he said that the 'personal stuff' was not his business.

'I don't need to know about how their weekends were or when their birthdays are,' he said. 'It is not important.'

All Julian wanted was for the team to function correctly and deliver what he expected them to deliver, but this clearly was not happening and for a very good reason. No one can expect people to come to work and not be complete human beings. His colleagues were not just their work and found it frustrating to be regarded in this way.

If, however, they'd believed that Julian cared about their welfare, they would have been more likely to embrace their roles and focus on the results they were getting. They'd also have been more willing to accept and act upon both praise and criticism if they were treated as individuals on a daily basis.[6] This is the most effective way to get people to deliver.

Julian was quite surprised when I explained this to him, but he got it eventually. Among a range of measures, we organised a joint coaching session with a member of the team who was having the most difficulty with the way things were going.

Julian's colleague was able to say, 'I find it really upsetting when you walk past me in the corridor and don't acknowledge me.' This was a revelation to Julian, who hadn't meant to be rude or offensive. He'd just never thought about it in this way.

Over time and with some effort, relationships in this department improved. Granted, Julian was a little bit wooden initially as he chatted informally with his colleagues, but with practice, he was able to create a noticeably better team spirit.

Julian's case is not an isolated one. There are plenty of scientific, logical people who are so focused on delivering their results that they don't understand the need to balance delivery with recognising people as people. I spoke to another client about building a better relationship with her team and she perfectly (albeit inadvertently) articulated the problem. After telling me that her priorities were on delivery and reaching her targets, she concluded that soft skills were not high on her agenda.

The label 'soft skills' is misleading, unhelpful and diminishes their importance. As John Sculley, the former president of PepsiCo, is commonly attributed to have said about the process of training people to build relationships and communications skills, 'Stop calling it soft skills. This stuff is hard.'

This is why I call them human skills. They are the essential leadership skills that got us through the pandemic and will support us as we navigate future changes. They will set us apart from technology and AI, which has not yet replaced our human feelings and emotions. As Mr Sculley says, they are *hard* and they require courage, but when they are developed, they create environments where we can bring our best selves to work.

John McCusker, Global Vice President of Talent Management, Bacardi

A few years back, a colleague of mine who was running a women in leadership session in Miami asked if I could give a talk about managing emotion and dealing with conflict. I responded that I was probably the worst person to ask at that time as I had recently divorced and I was learning to express on the outside what I was thinking or feeling on the inside, rather than just keeping things bottled up without addressing the issue.

She said I was probably the *best* person to talk about this topic because I was on a journey. She was completely right. I decided then to share my experiences in a public forum, because it would help normalise talking about when you're not OK, and did a forty-minute session on the issue of imposter syndrome. I followed this with a podcast series where I gave space to others to talk about their insecurities and their mental wellbeing.

When you get to the level I'm at, I feel people look at me not as John, but as John McCusker, global vice president of talent management. They think that I have my s**t together, rather than being John who gets up every day with a whole series of insecurities and challenges. I have good days and bad days, like everyone else.

> A short time ago, I had coffee with a colleague and, because we'd built confidence with one another, partly on the back of me speaking freely about my own challenges, she spoke openly about it being the first anniversary of the death of her father. I felt that she appreciated that I understood exactly where she was emotionally. It was completely OK for her to talk about it and that is as it should be. If you can't show that emotion in the workplace, where else can you show it? This is the normality I have been working to create.

Analysing your EQ

Developing EQ involves a multistage strategy. The starting point is to commit to the power of a team approach, which means embracing just how much can be achieved when human beings work well together. As leader, you then need to take a good, honest look at your own skills and work out where you currently are on the scale of high, low or unexpressed EQ to properly understand your leadership style. Which skill set do *you* believe is the more important to develop: relationships or results?

Products such as the 2.0 EQ test I mentioned earlier are designed to give you an accurate picture of your current attitude to EQ and, equally importantly, an overview of how others perceive their EQ. A test like this will clearly identify the areas where there is room for improvement. In the absence of taking the test right this moment, there are a few simple questions you can ask yourself. This gives a more simplified, but nevertheless useful opening overview of your own EQ levels.

- Do you believe yourself to be fairly self-aware?

- Do you feel comfortable sharing your emotions?

- Do you conduct regular one-to-one check-ins with team members where you're not just asking how the work is going or what the deliverables are, but also enquiring how individuals are feeling?

- Do you notice if any members of the team are not getting along with one another?

- If something has not gone well, do you review it in the context of taking the emotional pulse of what happened?

- Does your team feel confident to speak freely about failure as well as success?

If the answer to these questions is mostly no, you will need to work on your EQ.

To expand upon this process and build a fuller picture, ask yourself these questions that push you beyond yes or no answers. If it makes it easier for you, look upon this exercise as having an honest chat with yourself:

- What's your approach to expressing emotions?

- What feelings are you comfortable expressing?

- Are you more comfortable with certain feelings than others?

- Which is the emotion you are most uncomfortable with?

- When something feels uncomfortable, do you bottle your emotions or brood? Why?

- Do you find it easier to express your emotions at home or at work? Why?

- What's the most common reaction you get when you express emotions?

Ask yourself if you are the type of person who acts differently at the workplace and at home. There are some people who, once they're in a leadership position, take the deliberate step to move away from expressing their emotions in the workplace, fearing it could undermine their authority. Often individuals like this express a high degree of EQ when they're at home or with close friends, yet actively suppress this quality the moment they step through the door into their workplace.

Their argument is that it is essential for a leader to be calm and composed at all times, particularly in crisis situations. They think, *No one wants to see their leaders putting everything they are thinking out on show, panicking and saying, 'Oh help, what are we going to do?' That's not going to inspire trust.*

While witnessing a leader paralysed with fear would be concerning for any team, an outward display of steely calm in the face of impending disaster does look somewhat inauthentic. Similarly, when the person in charge brushes off a crisis and pretends everything is OK, it looks like they don't really understand the gravity of the situation or aren't taking it seriously. If leaders don't show up in a genuine way, their colleagues know it. We all have an inbuilt radar for when others are acting in a manner we perceive as fake.

Showing up as a complete human being

There are two sides to working with teams when it comes to leading with emotion. The first concerns how a leader monitors and displays their own emotions, with consideration to how their behaviour impacts others. The second concerns monitoring the emotional climate of those around them and deciphering the dynamics of the situation to help others properly express their own emotions.

We'll look at the most appropriate way for leaders to deal with their own emotions to begin with. In Chapter Three, we saw how emotions can be contagious. Often without us realising it, our emotions impact our general demeanour and have a knock-on effect on those around us. While potentially disruptive among a group of colleagues, this can have an even greater impact when a team leader is subject to huge emotional swings.

To understand how this might work, turn your thoughts to a specific instance which filled you with a flood of emotions. It doesn't have to be a big event, just something that happened and perhaps caught you off guard. What you are looking for here is to remember how you felt and how you responded.

To give you an idea, let me share something that happened to me. I was running a two-hour online training session for twenty people and, after one hour, I announced a five-minute coffee break. Each person on the call turned off their camera and the sea of faces I'd been speaking to disappeared.

During that five-minute pause, I quickly checked my messages and came across a really unpleasant email. I hadn't been expecting it at all and it upset me. Obviously, I am trained to deal with the flood of sadness, worry and anger that hit me at that moment, but even so, it was a shock. I realised that I was very distressed, yet I immediately had to go back online and finish off the training in a professional manner.

In this instance, I had to park my feelings to return to and deal with the problem later. I breathed through it and used anchoring techniques to bring myself back into the here and now, but it could easily have derailed my day and I could have delivered the rest of that training badly.

Do you have any examples of similar instances that derailed you for a moment? How did you react? More importantly, how did you come across to those who report to you when this happened?

STUDY: The ripple effect: emotional contagion and its influence on group behaviour[7]

It's long been known that panic spreads quickly, but how much do other emotions 'go viral' among a group and influence their subsequent thoughts and actions? Four groups of people were selected for this study and the same actor was placed in each group in a leadership role, but he behaved differently in each group. In group one, he was cheerful and upbeat. In group two, he was warm and calm. In group three, he was hostile and irritable, and in group four, he pretended to be depressed and morose.

There was a noticeable emotional reaction in each group which went beyond merely mimicking the facial expressions, body language and tone of voice of the group leader. In the groups where the actor had been hostile, irritable or depressed, there was less co-operation and more conflict than in the groups where the actor displayed energy-giving emotions. The members didn't manage their tasks as well as those in the other groups.

As the study above shows, leaders need to monitor how they display emotions because they are infectious. It is easy to 'catch' energy-sapping emotions.

Do you monitor how you come across to team members? During stressful periods, do you find yourself walking around the building with shoulders slumped and a big frown? If you have something on your mind, is it usual for you to try to get conversations over with as quickly as possible so you can get on with the matter in hand, meaning you talk in hurried, clipped tones? Do you sit in meetings with your arms folded, tapping your foot with impatience?

If any of these examples describes you, rest assured the team will pick up on your moods. Even if you are making a deliberate effort to say nice things to colleagues, your endeavours will be undermined by the way you conduct yourself. Without realising it, you will be conveying your full emotions loud and clear.

Nienke Mulder, Chief Human Resource Officer (CHRO), The Global Fund

Everybody has emotions. The challenge for any leader is, do they always show unfiltered emotions or do they run them through an intelligent lens before they openly share them?

I'm more than happy with tears at work, both mine and other people's, and the same with laughter and joy. However, I do need to be conscious of the impact I have on my team. If there is too much pure emotion coming out, I may unintentionally put a burden on other people.

As a leader, you have responsibility for your intent and the impact that you make. I apply a filter where possible to quickly check that the emotion I am expressing is not just me venting and releasing, but is also the right thing for others to receive.

It's important to add here that this is not an invitation to hide or bottle up energy-sapping emotions so no one knows the real you. As a leader, you can't be relentlessly positive all the time. You must show a range of emotions, but be aware of how you express energy-sapping ones such as anxiety, anger or sadness and deal with them in a way that is not damaging to the rest of the team.

If you need to, say, express that a direct report has made a mistake or let someone know that what they have done is not OK, find a suitable space and the right moment, which is definitely not just as the anger is rising. Ahead of time, use mindfulness exercises, alongside the regulating tools you've learned, to take the edge off any energy-draining emotions. Then, when you do have the tricky conversation, you can show up as a complete human being. The more you practise, the better you will be at dealing with complex situations and the more comfortable you will be about expressing your emotions.

Consider the example of Helen (not her real name) who had become increasingly frustrated at her junior colleague's habit of talking over her in meetings or interrupting her when she was in full flow. Rather than letting the situation build up to fever pitch and finally snapping at him during a meeting, Helen chose her moment. She asked her colleague to meet her for a coffee, and then told him how what he was doing was making her angry.

The two had previously got along well, she noted, but if the situation were to continue, it would inevitably negatively impact their relationship. The colleague listened carefully and admitted he hadn't realised he was acting in this way. It really helped that Helen had addressed the problem in a calm and respectful way, which meant it could be easily resolved.

Vulnerability

Leaders should not be afraid to occasionally display vulnerability with their team. Vulnerability is at the heart of human social connection. People don't perceive it as being weak or lacking control, but as a sign of courageousness, honesty and bravery.[8]

When you show vulnerability, people can connect with you. Vulnerability is reassuring and helps to build a genuine connection between you as a leader and your team, encouraging more authentic communications.

A classic and oft-quoted example of this concerns the Tylenol poisoning scandal in 1982.[9] This was a time before manufacturers placed sealant barriers on the top of medicine bottles. A number of deaths occurred after poison was slipped into a batch of Tylenol containers.

During a subsequent TV interview, Johnson & Johnson CEO Bill Weldon didn't just condemn the poisoning, but he talked emotionally with tears in his eyes about the tragedy. His openness about his sadness and pain, together with his tears, showed viewers that this person was truly authentic. When he said this would never happen again, the public believed him and didn't abandon the company for alternative medicine suppliers. Even hard-nosed city analysts were satisfied. Tylenol shares, which had dropped at the start of the crisis, rose sharply again.

This case exemplifies the right balance between showing a degree of vulnerability as a leader while at the same time maintaining trust and inspiration among the team. In other words, it is selective vulnerability. The spokesperson was respected because he opened up and shared emotions, but also because he suggested a solution at the same time.

The authenticity of the Tylenol scenario can be replicated in most situations (although tears are not always necessary). In response to a crisis, for example, a leader might gather the team together and say, 'Yes, we are experiencing a difficult situation and I'm worried about it, but I have trust in you guys. We have the competencies and skills to get through this. There's a way forward here and this is what I think it is.'

A statement like this, told with conviction, shows that a leader is in control and can cope, so they will not lose any respect from the team. They are realistic about their emotional response, but optimistic too. When there is no sugar-coating, hiding or being fake, the leader comes across as a human being as well as the boss. Equally importantly, it emphasises that this leader has full trust and faith in the team.

Those leaders who struggle with expressing their emotions in this way can develop their skills using storytelling techniques. This is where they tell a story about themselves or about something or someone that has moved them. It is a handy way to ease into expressing sometimes difficult emotions. When the story is compelling enough, it will do a lot of the heavy lifting in conveying who the leader really is and what moves them.

Say a leader needs to make some tough calls and convey them to the team. They might explain the issues in the context of previous tough calls, where the end result was worth the means.

For example: 'Let me share something with you. In my first post as a CEO, I faced some interesting challenges. We had just had a major product recall, turnover was down by 50% and we'd had an exodus of some key staff. . .'

When a leader shares something personal in this way, the team will automatically feel more invested in what they have to say.

Michael A Piker, Global DE&I and Reward Director, Flutter Entertainment

If I can emotionally connect with people from the outset, it really helps. The way to truly recognise people is through storytelling, thanking them publicly or taking an interest in them on a personal level.

When people are impacted emotionally, they lose a sense of belonging and it's important as a leader to acknowledge that they are facing personal challenges every day. This is far more powerful and effective at keeping them engaged than just relying on monetary reward. Financial rewards can improve productivity, but may not always achieve engagement given the different perspectives of the people we work with and for.

If you are not a natural storyteller, you can practise by telling a story to family members or friends or colleagues you're close to. It's a good opportunity to experiment with how to tell the story and present the emotional element. Try telling it in different ways to see how each variation impacts the listener. Focus too on the tone you tell it in, as well as the body language you use.

While some leaders do much of this naturally, not all will find showing vulnerability easy at first. As with so many of the techniques outlined in this book, the answer is in practice. Take it step by step.

Creating a culture of emotional safety

For any leader thinking about their EQ, managing the emotional climate of the whole team is just as important as how they personally behave at work. They may have mastered the art of displaying emotions and remaining largely happy and positive, but the rest of the team may not.

Some may argue that leaders cannot constantly monitor the emotions of their teams and that it can be counterproductive to try, getting in the way of actual leadership. The train of thought goes something like this: 'Leaders need to be decisive and take action. If they were to pay constant attention to how their teams were feeling, they would not get very far.'

There is a balance to be had. In certain situations, such as a crisis or during a critical part of a project, it may be that the leader must indeed focus on taking action and not base their decisions around the emotions of the team. However, there will be many situations where monitoring the emotional climate of the team will be vital and will, in fact, provide the leader with information that is central to that team's motivation, morale and productivity.

In the office

Emotionally intelligent leaders must continually take the emotional pulse of their teams. This is an essential first stage in recognising if individuals around them are not doing well or showing signs of anger, sadness, fear or any of the other energy-draining emotions. It will help leaders become aware of when the behaviour of a particular member of the team changes. Maybe one individual has become withdrawn, isolating themselves from colleagues and no longer taking part in social events. Perhaps they are not taking breaks or holidays, or are putting on or losing weight. Monitoring the emotional pulse of a team also means leaders can quickly deal with any potential conflict situations, say where two team members are not getting along or a particular person is upsetting all their colleagues.

These warning signs are easy to observe if you are looking out for them. It requires regularly checking in with the team and having conversations about their perspective on events. It is easy to assume that everyone will react in just the same way that you do or think in the exact same way. They don't and that is why these regular take-the-pulse sessions are so useful.

I saw an excellent example of this in action early on in the COVID-19 pandemic. Immediately prior to the crisis, a division of a large IT firm had been busily preparing to host a high-profile international conference. As is common with these events, months of planning had been done, requiring many thousands of people hours.

Then virtually overnight, the conference was cancelled as countries all over the world went into lockdown. There was no certainty the conference would ever happen at all or, if it did, when that might be. Naturally, the entire team was devastated.

The director of the division got the team together and asked them this simple yet crucial question: 'How are you feeling?' He encouraged the team members to respond by explaining how sad and disappointed he was by the turn of events. He too had been working hard to make this conference a success and the news was a big blow.

The combination of his rapid response to an unforeseen event that brought the mood of the whole team down along with his authenticity encouraged everyone to voice how they felt. It helped the entire team to get their own reactions to the setback out of their systems and they all really appreciated the IT director's support. After giving everyone a chance to vent, he went on to talk about some of the projects they could all still look forward to, which again proved hugely motivational.

Impromptu meetings like this are crucial during difficult times, because they provide team members with much-needed emotional support and recognition that they may not be feeling upbeat about what is happening. However, these meetings shouldn't simply be reserved for the tough times. It is still far too rare to find organisations with a culture where people are regularly encouraged to talk about how they feel, particularly if energy-sapping emotions are involved.

There is a misguided belief that if we discuss anger or sadness, it might undermine the happiness in the rest of the organisation, getting in the way of the more rational, logical approach that powers that organisation. The opposite is, in fact, true, so make a frequent habit of checking in to ask everyone in your teams how they feel.

Among a hybrid team

Xiangchen Zhang, Deputy Director-General, World Trade Organization (WTO)

We have to get used to this hybrid working model, where people work at home for a few days a week. In some circumstances, there is much to be said for homeworking because it presents a more efficient environment for certain tasks. If, for example, a colleague has a large report to write, it is better for them to do it at home where it is quiet and there are less distractions.

However, there is merit to office life too. People are more likely to chat together there and make a real emotional connection. It is a working environment, but also a place where people can relax with one another and that makes people happy.

> One area where I believe that a presence in the office is essential is for negotiations. If you don't have that human contact, you will not get the best outcome. Not that long ago, I saw a real example of this. We were in our green room, a breakout area where people on all sides of a negotiation can have informal chats. I saw two ministers from different countries talking together quietly and, just before they parted, one minister gently patted the arm of the other. Both ministers left the room with their delegations and returned twenty minutes later to say they had reached an agreement. The negotiation had been deadlocked before, but this short private conversation made all the difference.
>
> We need to pay attention to the value of personal contact. Some emotional connections are more effective when you are in the same room.

The most significant change in the move to hybrid working isn't related to geography. This is the first time leaders have become properly aware of their employees as whole people.

When we view one another on screens, we see into other people's homes and get glimpses of their personal lives. We see a human side to our colleagues that we were never really aware of when they simply turned up to the office each day. That clear boundary between work and home is gone. We can't ignore the whole person any longer. This means team leaders need to make an additional effort to connect with their teams on an emotional basis and get an idea of what is happening with them.

At a basic level, this may mean being more accommodating to the clear pressures of juggling family life with work, which is something that is long overdue, anyhow. Now personal arrangements have come into play, leaders need to provide a safety net. The decision on what days employees work from home or which hours they work can be weighed against childcare responsibilities rather than made solely around the previously rigid rules of the workplace. The same goes for an employee who may need to visit an elderly parent in a care home.

Leaders need to help their teams feel safe to talk more about their personal lives and not feel like they are being judged for it. The checking-in process I just described must be much more intentional and deliberate than it ever has been to make up for the physical distance between team members. With the opportunity to bump into someone in the corridor gone, leaders need to schedule time to have informal exchanges.

Checking-in chats should include opportunities for people to talk about what is going on at home. All meetings, whether in person or online, could begin by the leader gauging the emotional pulse of everyone present. They can encourage discussion of previously off-limit subjects such as challenges with school arrangements or health issues.

The goal of these checking-in sessions is to create a connection. Starting an online meeting with a 'Hi, how are you all?' is fine, but it should go beyond this. Team leaders could ask, 'On a scale of one to ten, what is your energy level right now?' or 'What were you up to before the meeting?' or 'Name an emotion you are feeling this morning.' If the meeting is with a large group, the leader can introduce a facility for team members to submit answers anonymously. This is a great way to take the temperature of the team.

At the end of the meeting, the leader could extend an open invitation for everyone to hang around for ten minutes for a catch-up chat over a virtual coffee. Once again, it is a process of recreating the physical experience, but it will only happen if the leader does it intentionally.

Nienke Mulder, CHRO, The Global Fund

When we start meetings, I always ask my team members to hold up their hands to give a 'best of five', showing how they feel today as per the number of fingers. It makes a difference.

When I was late to a meeting one time, the team immediately asked me why I hadn't put my hand up. I had to tell them that I didn't know how I felt at that moment. It had been a day of highs and lows, so it was hard to put a number on it, but we were all aware of the importance of this process.

I also always ask, 'Do you need any support with anything?' It can be practical or emotional help. Most of the time, they say no, but the opportunity for them to speak up is there and/or we can follow up with an individual conversation.

There will, of course, need to be some boundaries. Leaders who have not until now been in the habit of encouraging members of the team to talk openly might introduce the new regime by asking everyone how they'd like to discuss emotions. What's OK and what's not OK? Does there need to be a team charter of what's in and what's out?

The goal is to make it normal for everyone to talk about emotions and establish the workplace as a place of emotional safety. Emotional safety is where people can express their feelings to each other and to their bosses without any worries that they're going to be reprimanded or seen in a poor light for doing so, or that it might jeopardise their respect from their colleagues. This by no means implies a leader needs to become a skilled counsellor or psychologist. They simply have to create a space to make expressing emotions an important part of company culture.

When the team is setting out these unwritten rules, it is useful to make it clear how everyone will work together in a fair, balanced way. Is it, for example, OK for one person to turn their screen off in a meeting with twenty colleagues who keep their screens on? Similarly, what is the policy on people checking emails during an online meeting? When the camera is on, it is clear when they are doing this. If it is allowed to happen without comment, it can undo a lot of the good work the leader is doing through the checking-in session because it throws connection and trust out of the window. Needless to say, it is even worse when the boss is scrolling through their messages when they should be giving their team their full attention.

Leaders need to think about body language when they're speaking with their team face to face. So much of the information that we communicate to others is done through means other than the words we say. In fact, as little as 10% of our communication is conveyed through speech;[10] the rest is nonverbal through body language, gesture, tone, voice and expression, and the screen can really amplify these non-verbal clues.

Leaders must be aware of how they come across in the virtual world. If they rush from one meeting to another and look frazzled and distracted, the rest of the team will pick up on it. It creates tension and impacts the tone of the meeting. To stop this happening, even on a hectic day, it is well worth taking the time to briefly reflect on your physical and emotional state before turning the camera on.

Leaders also need to be aware that while some people flourish working at home, others don't. I'm an extrovert by nature and know I sometimes find it challenging to sit alone behind a computer all day. I need to see people and I find face to face interactions energising.

Through my coaching work, I have discovered that introverts generally warm to the homeworking environment and relish the independence. Leaders need to identify which members of their team are extroverts and who the introverts are and have empathy with the situation of each group. They may need to check in with the introverts more regularly than the extroverts, possibly inviting them into the office more often for in-person meetings.

If the team is relatively small, leaders could schedule one day a week or month where everyone is in the office at the same time. A virtual open-door policy via Slack, WhatsApp or Snapchat is also helpful, so extrovert team members can communicate more easily and say when they are having a bad day. (For more ideas on this, turn to Chapter Ten).

For introverts, you as leader can encourage hybrid workers to contribute during occasional team get-togethers by sharing meeting notes and agendas a few days ahead of time. This gives them much-needed time and space to think about what they will want to say. During online meetings, it may help to offer the option for them to comment in writing via the chat function, so they don't need to 'take the floor' and speak to the whole group. Make sure that online meetings are not held back-to-back throughout the day, so everyone gets a little time in between to recharge their batteries.

It is tempting to think that hybrid or remote working is easy since there is no longer a daily commute, but this isn't necessarily true. It can be very tiring. When we go into the office five days a week, there is a routine and a rhythm. We get up at the same time, have coffee breaks at the same time and leave the office at the same time. Working at home is completely different. Our schedules are much less settled and this can be emotionally draining.

According to one survey, 80% of leaders reported that hybrid working is exhausting for employees.[11]

Meanwhile, 20% of workers reported difficulties in switching off from work and struggling with feeling always on. Leaders need to help their teams adjust and introduce measures to reduce stress. The check-in process will highlight who is struggling.

Once you've established a safe emotional space, the team will respond quickly and positively. There will be a marked willingness to speak up about issues and put forward new ideas. Indeed, one poll found increasing emotional safety in the workplace can lead to a 12% boost in productivity.[12] For employees to be fully engaged, their leaders need to bring their full selves to work, and then put measures in place to encourage everyone else to do the same.

Summary

In this chapter, we have explored the importance of a leader having EQ. One of the clear trends of the Great Resignation is employees are leaving businesses (and business leaders) that don't care to join ones that do care.

It's impossible to be a successful leader today without EQ. People are people, not just machines employed to do a job, so we all need to make the effort to treat each other as such in the workplace. After all, more than anything, it'll be EQ that sets us humans apart from AI.

SIX
Leading With Empathy

Empathy is powerful because it neutralises energy-sapping emotions. When one person is frustrated, angry or dissatisfied and another hears them out or offers constructive, helpful solutions, it softens those feelings, which can threaten to overwhelm, and paves the way to finding an equitable solution to the problem.

Of all the essential EQ skills, empathy is the most crucial, which is why I've devoted an entire chapter to it. It's the secret to understanding why individuals are the way they are and connecting with them. Business leaders need empathy to build trust.

Empathy is basically being able to put yourself in another person's shoes and feel their emotion. It doesn't mean that you agree with them 100%, but you do *get it*.

STUDY: Mirror neurons[1]

One of the most important discoveries about mirror neurons was made by observing macaque monkeys. A group of psychologists at the University of Palma placed electrodes in a monkey's brain to record neural activity, hoping to find out more about how the brain orchestrates simple movements of the hand.

They found, as expected, neurons that fired specifically when the macaques performed particular actions. However, those neurons also fired when the macaques observed the experimenters eating lunch in the same room. When the researchers picked up the food and gave it to the monkeys, the same neurons fired. This highlighted the existence of mirror neurons: brain cells that fired both when the monkey performed an activity and when someone else did it.

That's the basis of empathy. It explains how we can mirror and be in touch with what's happening with other people and empathise when they are happy, sad or frustrated. If, say, we were to see somebody who's struggling or in pain and our brain were to be scanned at that exact moment, the pain part would light up. We are meant to be empathetic and compassionate.

The value of empathy

The previous chapter highlighted why EQ is so important today; important enough, in fact, that people are actively changing jobs to seek out businesses that value emotional skills. Empathy, or a lack of empathy, is a driver of this trend and has a significant impact in a range of scenarios.

According to the Lady Geek Global Empathy Index, the top ten most empathetic companies outperform the bottom ten by 50%.[2] In another study, employees with highly empathetic bosses report higher levels of creativity (61%) and engagement (76%) versus those with less empathetic leaders (13% and 32% respectively).[3] When it comes to retention, 57% of white women and 62% of women of colour said that they were unlikely to think of leaving their companies when they felt that they were respected and valued by those companies. Meanwhile, in the area of inclusivity, 50% of people with empathetic leaders reported their workplace was inclusive, compared with only 17% of those with the less empathetic leaders. Hardly surprisingly, those organisations at the top of the empathy index routinely appear on the lists of most desirable employers to work for.

Millennials and Gen Z, the digital natives, are leading the way by voting with their feet. People from these generations are forecast to have more than twenty jobs over their working lives.[4] This is many times the number of previous generations, who may work for just four or five firms.

Just as businesses don't offer jobs for life, workers today don't offer unquestioning commitment. In fact, Millennials are quite prepared to swaps jobs to find meaning. They are much more flexible, much less tethered than previous generations, and they want empathy. This generation is also three times more likely to be comfortable talking about their emotions than previous generations.[5]

More than half of employees are leaving their jobs because they are looking for work more aligned with their personal values.[6] Firms that don't recognise this face a rapid turnover of staff.

Whatever way you look at it, whether you're measuring growth, earnings or productivity, there is value in empathy. You'd therefore be forgiven for imagining employers would be tripping over themselves to build empathy into every corner of their organisation. While many are, a lot are getting it very wrong. One telling analysis of language patterns in public job posts for prominent tech companies found there has been a noticeable rise in phrases such as 'world-class', 'fast-paced', 'aggressive' and 'discipline'.[7] Meanwhile, words such as 'flexible', 'empathy' and 'belonging' are falling out of favour.

CEOs in all sectors say they understand the importance of empathy, but consistently overestimate their own skill and that of their organisation in exhibiting the quality. This is reflected in surveys, with one report showing 92% of CEOs say their organisations are empathetic versus 72% of employees saying they work for an empathetic employer, and that employee figure is falling.[8] In some cases, this is because leaders simply don't know how to be empathetic. Another study showed a decline in empathetic skills of between 34% and 48% over an eight-year period.[9]

There is no doubt that our increasing reliance on tech and machine learning is pushing aside empathy. Indeed, for all its grand promises of democratisation, technology is fuelling an *empathy deficit*. A perfect example of how this happens, albeit inadvertently, can be found in the early attempts at building facial-recognition software.

The Silicon Valley experts who coded such technology, often young white and Asian men, had their own biases. This became apparent in the first versions of these programs because they demonstrated noticeable biases in both skin-type and gender. Error rates in determining the gender of light-skinned men were never even as high as 1%.[10] For dark-skinned women, error rates soared to more than 34% in some programs.

Another classic example of how easy it is to introduce biases into data sets comes courtesy of Microsoft. Its 2016 attempt at engaging Millennials with a tweet chatbot backfired within hours of its launch. The idea had been to improve customer service, but users flooded it with misogynistic and racist remarks, which the AI machine learned and started regurgitating back within forty-eight hours.

With our businesses ever more reliant on technology, it is easy to see how a single biased individual can easily create wide-reaching damage. All the town hall meetings and get-to-know-you chats in the world won't make a jot of difference in creating an environment of empathy if vast numbers in an organisation feel singled out and excluded.

Technology contributes to another factor that is almost certainly involved in fuelling an empathy deficit: an ever-faster pace of working. Everyone is expected to do more, and more quickly, especially in the tough post-COVID trading environment. Interestingly, some companies did manage to strike an empathetic tone during the pandemic, but these changes were in many cases only temporary. With more and more being heaped on the plates of leaders, they feel the need to limit face-to-face conversations. Empathy is seen as more of a nice-to-have rather than a key tool to expedite growth.

There is possibly a gender divide at play here too. The growth in headlines critical of 'toxic masculinity' and 'mansplaining' and tendency for social media to brutally call out examples of perceived gender bias have had the knock-on effect of encouraging some male leaders to say as little as possible to female reports for fear of saying the wrong thing. Meanwhile, some women shy away from any corporate programmes that aim to promote an even playing field, concerned that participating might make them look weak or single them out as getting special treatment.

Even though this is pure perception and our actions may be subconscious, it means both men and women are getting into a habit of deliberately concealing their true behaviour and suppressing empathy to keep the peace. Continually second-guessing what others may or may not think of our words and actions is not a healthy state of affairs and definitely does more harm than good. While empathy should unite us and help us to work together and recognise the strengths of every individual, it seems many organisations are falling well short of this goal.

Leading an empathetic organisation

When you're establishing empathy to build strong teams, it helps to know that there are three distinct categories which intensify progressively:

1. **Cognitive** empathy: *I understand you.* (If I was in their position, what would I be thinking right now?)

2. **Effective** empathy. *I feel for you.* (Being in their position would make me feel. . .)

3. **Compassionate** empathy. *I understand, I feel and I want to help.* (I am going to act now.)

There is a lot of talk nowadays around compassion and how this is the behaviour leaders should strive for. The foundation of the word 'compassion' comes from the Latin *compati*, which means 'suffering together'. Compassion is where leaders not only see what concerns individuals on their team, but are inclined to go one step further and act upon it as well, do something to help.

Those empathetic leaders who get it right, compared with those who don't, are:

- Better and more effective at making decisions and doing so more quickly

- More sensitive and open to the opinions and views of others

- Curious and listen more

- More effective at communicating and connecting with the team

- Willing to increase their influence and impact

Empathy is *not* a catch-all endorsement of poor job performance, come what may, or a charter to agree 100% with everything being said. The goal is to walk in another's shoes, even for a short time, and suspend any prejudice brought about from one's own perspective to understand a situation from another's vantage point. This in turn opens the way to responding fairly and equitably without being judgmental or exasperated by differing viewpoints.

Despite all the known positive impacts of empathy, many business leaders clearly struggle with displaying it. One study found that only a quarter of employees felt there was enough empathy in their workplaces,[11] while another found that 62% of workers worried their bosses would judge them negatively for taking time out for their mental health.[12] Often, those in a leadership position worry that they will be less respected if they show empathy, with seven in ten admitting that they find it hard to show this in the office.[13]

Like EQ, empathy is a quality which some people *think* they are good at, when they are not. They'll mistakenly believe: *I'm a kind person, I must be empathetic.* While they may indeed think kind thoughts, they may not be acting upon them or showing any emotion. There is a world of difference between being kind and showing it. Again, a more accurate measure of empathy can be achieved with an EQ test.

A shortage of empathy is not just a problem in the day-to-day operation of a business; it's particularly damaging if empathy is ignored during any crisis situation. This is a time where leaders need to tune into the fears and worries of their staff, and then do something about it.

Pausing in a crisis to consider how the team is coping can, of course, be challenging because it's when we're least open to being compassionate and empathetic. There is so much to think about, so many solutions to juggle, but it's also the moment where it's absolutely crucial not to get entirely caught up in the logistics. The wider picture needs attention too.

Developing your empathy muscle

Empathy, like charity, starts at home. The goal here is to develop the frontal insula, which is the part of the brain where we sense love and hate, gratitude and resentment, self-confidence and embarrassment, and empathy. Like any muscle, if we exercise the frontal insula regularly, we will strengthen what it does, which in this case is being increasingly empathetic.

The good news is, developing your empathy muscle is a lot less arduous than hitting the gym; it's as simple as being kind to yourself. Self-compassion is vital before you can be compassionate to others.

Think of treating yourself in the same way as you would treat your best friend. This doesn't mean be easy on yourself or complacent; it just means that you acknowledge yourself for who you are and what you do. Make an effort to be positive about what is going on around you, give yourself some compliments and make a point of forgiving yourself for any past mistakes. Take some time to make a mental list of all your strengths and capabilities to give yourself a boost.

Finally, don't forget to reward yourself from time to time. Do something you enjoy that makes you feel like you. Maybe it's a massage or a round of golf or settling down with a nice book. The choice is yours. By prioritising yourself, you'll be in a better place to look after other people. Self-compassion develops your resilience.

Mindfulness exercises are another useful tool in developing that empathy muscle. Once you have become more mindful of how you speak and what you say, consider where you may not be showing enough compassion to yourself. Individuals who do not consider their own selves find it hard to be compassionate towards others.

Once you are in a compassionate frame of mind, have a look around your organisation. Are there any practices and policies that, on reflection, don't seem very compassionate? What can you as a leader do to change this?

Active listening

HumanForce has carried out a number of high-level assessments on listening in the workplace and in nearly every survey, the feedback we get is along the lines of 'My boss doesn't listen correctly' or 'I don't feel that my boss has any time to listen to my concerns.' If this is the case in any organisation, it can become a company-wide trend.

Active listening is one of the main tools in fostering a culture of empathy and compassion. When we don't listen and the other person sees that or feels like they're not being heard, that is not empathetic at all.

We are all guilty of not listening properly at some time or another. Perhaps you will recognise some of these ten blocks to active listening and know you engage in one or two yourself:

1. **Mind reading.** Assuming we already know what the person is thinking and feeling without asking.

2. **Rehearsing.** Sometimes, when people are talking, we are already rehearsing or mentally planning out what we are going to say next. This means we miss what's really being said.

3. **Multitasking.** Performing another task while the person is talking, such as glancing at a new message on our phone.

4. **Judging.** Evaluating what the speaker is saying according to our own beliefs.

5. **Daydreaming.** Getting lost in our own thoughts.

6. **Advising.** Rushing to give suggestions and solutions rather than just listening.

7. **Undervaluing.** Reframing a situation in a positive way by saying, 'Don't worry, it will be fine' or 'Life is good!'

8. **Being right.** Resisting any information that means we ourselves need to change.

9. **Defensive.** We must be right at all costs.

10. **Derailing.** Where the other person talks and we think about something that relates to us and interrupt with our own story.

In all cases, we are not actively engaging with our interlocutor. We are either practising *internal listening*, where we are looking at another person and pretending to listen, but are actually preoccupied with our own internal thoughts, or *focused listening*, meaning we are focused on what the person is saying, but not properly engaging with or feeling the emotion that they're trying to convey.

What we need to train ourselves to do is *active listening*. This is 360-degree listening where we're not just focusing on what the other person *is* saying, but also on what they are *not* saying. In other words, we are feeling the vibes in the room, paying attention to body language and all the other nonverbal cues regarding the person's emotional state.

Active listening requires us to be attentive, to understand what someone is saying so we can respond and retain information. When we listen actively, we establish trust, show empathy and create a place of psychological safety. The person being listened to will feel that they're cared about.

The first step in active listening is to pay attention. This means getting into the right zone. If you need to have an important conversation, it would be counterproductive to rush into it, squeezing it in between two meetings. Instead, schedule some time at the beginning or end of the day when you and your interlocutor are both in the right frame of mind. Then, be sure to listen with an open mind.

The second step is to show that you've listened well and you fully understand. A useful technique here is to reframe what the other person has said.

Your response could be: 'If I've heard you right, you are saying. . .' Mirroring shows that you've really listened properly and gets rid of any concerns that you're simply assuming you've got everything right. Perhaps also finish with: 'Is my understanding correct?'

Once again, remember that your response is conveyed by more than just words. Think about your tone of voice and facial expression. Body language is key. The most obvious sign that you are listening is nodding, but make sure to face your body towards the speaker and don't glance away.

Sameer Chauhan, Director of United Nations International Computing Centre (UNICC)

Sometimes, active listening means taking feedback, even if it is unpleasant. It shows you get where other people are coming from. When nothing is off limits, it creates an environment of psychological safety.

> There was an incident with a member of the team who came to a meeting absolutely fuming. We'd given her an application that we'd been building far too early because she'd previously said she wanted to start testing right away. It wasn't ready and we shouldn't have let it happen. She spent forty minutes venting and, when she stopped, we held our hands up and said she was absolutely right, we shouldn't have released it to her when it was not ready.
>
> 'We are good techies, but bad communicators,' we said. She needed to know we had genuinely heard her. We gave the app to her a week later, when it was ready, and the relationship was already much better.

With remote teams, active listening can be harder than it is face to face as we may suffer from screen fatigue after too many virtual meetings have sapped our energy. In addition, technical issues such as screen freezes can distract us and interrupt our ability to be fully present with another person.

With these challenges, leaders need to make an extra effort to ensure that empathy is maintained. Many of the steps outlined in the section on hybrid teams in the previous chapter, such as keeping cameras on and being mindful of non-verbal cues, will make a huge difference here.

Another useful tool in displaying empathy is asking for permission. This comes into its own in a situation where we are about to give advice or feedback, or perhaps need to have a delicate conversation with somebody who has been struggling. Going straight into it with a statement like, 'I'm just going to give you some feedback' is likely to send the person on the other end of this statement straight into fight, flight or freeze mode.

(There are exceptions to this: the streaming service Netflix encourages feedback all the time, so it has become an accepted part of normal day-to-day office life. Colleagues will pass on feedback in front of anyone and everyone at meetings or in the hallway, or at any moment. It is built into the culture, so there is no stigma that goes with it.)[14]

We all get anxious when somebody's about to say something critical or unexpectedly initiates a conversation that's delicate and sensitive. When we are defensive, we become closed and unreceptive, which means nothing will go in properly. This response makes it impossible to subsequently have a good conversation.

Asking for permission lessens the emotional intensity of the situation. It helps your interlocutor feel considered, listened to and consequently more receptive to what you say.

You could say: 'I have some thoughts about this, can I share them with you?' or 'Are you open to me sharing some thoughts and hearing where I'm coming from?' or 'Would it be OK for us to have a conversation about this?'

Open questions

As the conversation progresses, consider the way that you ask questions. Open questions are much more powerful for getting people to speak freely than closed ones. Closed questions like the two below invite a simple yes or no answer and therefore don't gather much information:

- Are you feeling OK?

- Has this project been completed?

Open questions, on the other hand, make people stop and dig deep, and they invite introspection. They also show that the person's responses are of interest to you and that you'll listen to them. Open questions start with what, when and how.

These five simple questions are extremely effective in getting to the core of a challenge:

1. What is happening with you right now?

2. What's next?

3. What about that is important to you?

4. What else?

5. What do you need?

While sometimes uncomfortable to hear, each question invites a full response and indicates that you are curious about the other person's point of view. These powerful questions are real coaching tools which may stop people in their tracks, so you need to give them time for a response.

When you're asking open questions, take care not to couch them in words that sound like you are making a prejudgement of the response. Examples of leading questions to avoid include:

- Why haven't you. . .?

- Why do you always. . .?

- Have you thought about. . .?

- Why are you failing at. . .?

- What is the problem here?

- Don't you know better than. . .?

- Wouldn't you agree that. . .?

The aim is to create a culture where active listening is the norm. This will move any organisation towards being more empathetic. Small yet significant shifts have the power to transform the workplace and we've never needed them more than we do today.

Balancing empathy and accountability

While the values and virtues of empathy are crucial, employees are still at work to do a job. There is a balance to be had between empathy and accountability, but when team leaders show empathy, it becomes easier for them to encourage accountability.

I recently came across an example where a team leader showed empathy and compassion to a direct report whose dog had just died, allowing her to work at home for a couple of days. This did not prevent him from giving some constructive feedback on an issue she hadn't handled well on her return to the office, but he believed that she took the feedback positively because he had previously shown empathy.

It is clearly a difficult line to walk, though. Many business leaders I have spoken with have expressed some concern about how far to go either way. If, say, they are too kind and empathetic, then their teams might not do everything they're supposed to do. On the other hand, if they are too concerned about results, then they'll lose the support of their teams.

The aftermath of the pandemic brought this need for balance into sharp focus. During this difficult time, many leaders were under pressure because they felt that they had to show they really cared. Their empathetic muscle was flexed more than usual when many of their staff struggled with all sorts of challenges.

Now the pandemic is behind us, I've heard some business leaders saying that they believe they're being taken advantage of. They now feel under pressure to continue to grant flexible work arrangements and are uncomfortable about complaints from team members if they're told that they'll have to work, say, three days a week in the office rather than two days.

These leaders want to know, what are the boundaries? At what point do they need to be empathetic and at what point is it OK to put their foot down? How do they hold the team accountable to get the work done?

It's a tricky situation and understanding and respecting where the team is coming from is still crucial, but it doesn't mean that those in charge have to put kindness first all the time. Tough decisions still need to be taken.

Say, for example, there needs to be redundancies. The economic situation is tough and it is impossible to maintain employee numbers at their present level. Making people redundant may seem particularly difficult in the aftermath of an event such as COVID-19, because bosses will inevitably think about all that employees have gone through over the last few years, but the business still needs to function. In this case, team leaders will need to ensure everything is fair in the dismissal process and the employees involved have adequate coaching and feedback to help them overcome any obstacles they now face.

In less final situations than redundancy, it is still important to be clear on boundaries and to make sure that everybody knows exactly what they're supposed to be doing. A clarity of expectation will ensure every employee knows that they're going to be held accountable. They will be given opportunities to ask questions, talk about things when they're facing challenges and have an ongoing dialogue, but they also have an objective to reach at the end of each day. Leaders need to make it clear what the boundaries are and what things are non-negotiable.

When they have to take important decisions, team leaders may need to distance themselves from the emotions of the team under their control. They can show they are empathetic and understand the emotions involved, but also make it clear they have to make the decisions. This may mean stepping back, gathering information and taking time to properly consider the circumstances.

Leaders also need to look out for team members who are constantly negative and complaining because they can drain the energy of the whole team. In this case, it might be prudent for leaders to say they've listened to these team members and heard their point of view, but politely add that they don't have time to listen to them all the time. This clearly sets how much time they can give to each team member. Not everyone will be happy about this, but leaders need to make such decisions to move forward.

Building an empathy wall

Rubén Alejandro, Group Head Diversity and Inclusion, Syngenta Group

It is important to learn how to lead with emotions, but also how to identify and accept our own emotions. We need to recognise when our own mental health is not at its best and learn how to handle this in the workplace.

This all hinges on how well you know or even love yourself. We are all human and need to be able to connect with our emotions.

As Rubén says, leaders mustn't allow themselves to be swallowed up by the emotions of everyone on their team. Those in a position of responsibility must create an emotional wall within themselves.

This is a skill I have learned as a coach. While I need to show those I work with a lot of empathy, I make a conscious effort not to be overcome by their emotions. This means making sure I leave some space for me.

It is not healthy to take on everyone's burdens as well as your own. You need to detach yourself from this and set limits, which means learning how to stand back, judge objectively and act in the right way. I recommend that everyone in a position of leadership recognises the difference between how other people are feeling and how they themselves are feeling, and gives themselves time to step away from other people's emotions.

There are warning signs for leaders to look out for which show there may be cracks in their empathy wall. Some of the common signs that showing too much empathy is impacting a leader's assertiveness, morale and effectiveness include:

- Seeking too much input and procrastinating when taking a decision

- Feeling drained by the strong emotions shown by others

- Avoiding difficult decisions which may be unpopular

To avoid any of the above happening, leaders need to step back and find time to take stock of what is happening. They must be clear in their own minds about how much input they need from their teams for decision making and when to take certain decisions without the consensus of others. Learning how to deal with anxiety or negativity in the team is crucial, as is being able to set boundaries on how much and how often they listen to their people.

It is a key skill for a leader to learn how to 'feel' with people without being disturbed by their problems. This doesn't mean moving towards becoming detached and aloof, but rather being involved to a reasonable extent while not getting completely immersed in the problems of individual team members.

Leaders must establish the boundaries between themselves and others. Ultimately, recognising the difference between the feelings of the team and their own feelings will help them to establish this balance. All of this takes time and practice.

Summary

Of all the essential EQ skills, empathy is the most crucial. Business leaders need empathy to build connection and trust.

Empathy is powerful because it neutralises energy-sapping emotions. When one person is frustrated, angry or dissatisfied and another hears them out, it softens those feelings and paves the way to finding an equitable solution to the problem.

SEVEN

Holding Delicate And Difficult Conversations

I'd been coaching a client – let's call her Amy – for a while when, during one session, she mentioned that she was about to have a difficult conversation with somebody on the team who had been underperforming. Amy was a person who never enjoyed having difficult conversations and had always shied away from them in the past. She'd been working on her EQ, but it didn't come easily to her.

What, I asked her, was she doing to prepare for this conversation? She gave me a broad smile, dug into her bag and pulled out a folded piece of paper, which she passed across to me.

It was clear this piece of paper had been unfolded and refolded many times as Amy no doubt added to it and read and re-read it. After carefully unfolding it, I understood everything. It was a carefully written list of all the issues Amy had with the person she was about to speak with. Even though each bullet point contained just a few words, it was easy to see that each one was referring to some sort of perceived shortcoming in her colleague. It was quite a substantial list too.

'Do you think this is the best approach?' I asked, picking my words carefully. Amy shrugged.

'I expect this conversation isn't going to go well,' she said. 'I thought it would help to be prepared, so I wrote down all of the incidents I might need to prove my point.'

I couldn't help but reflect that it was as though Amy was preparing for a battle rather than a serious conversation. While Amy's meticulous approach was unusual, her fears about the task ahead of her were not. Study after study has shown that employees avoid tough conversations at work.

In an online Interact survey by Harris Poll, which included more than 600 managers, 69% said they were often uncomfortable communicating with other members of the team.[1] When it comes to telling colleagues how they are doing, 37% said they were uncomfortable giving any sort of direct feedback about performance, particularly if they thought someone might respond negatively to the feedback.

What is perhaps most worrying is that there is no sign this situation is improving. One organisation conducted a survey in 2009 and found that 70% of employees were avoiding the tough conversations.[2] It repeated the exercise ten years later and this figure hadn't budged at all.

Leaders are shying away from difficult conversations for a multitude of reasons. Perhaps they've had previous experience where these conversations have escalated into conflict because their direct report out-and-out rejected the feedback. At the other end of the scale, perhaps they've judged their previous endeavours as making zero difference to the employee's performance. Building themselves up for the tough conversation was a waste of time. Maybe, they have a bad memory of a person they were speaking with completely crumbling in front of them because they couldn't handle the perceived criticism.

The factor that unites this reluctance to act is emotions or, more specifically, energy-draining emotions such as fear, sadness, shame or disappointment. Since these are emotions that we can't avoid when we're having difficult conversations, we distance ourselves from the whole idea.

Does this matter? Yes, it does. It is a leader's job to develop their team and to help their colleagues to be the best they can be. Sometimes, that means having difficult conversations about under-performance or poor behaviour, otherwise the leader's job is only half done. Team members won't learn from their mistakes or see areas where they can improve.

Most importantly of all, employees *want* to have these conversations. They welcome feedback from leaders, managers and peers. These insights have the potential to advance their abilities and future career and are therefore highly valued. In fact, poll data shows that employees who receive meaningful feedback are almost four times more engaged than those who don't.[3]

The key word to focus on here is 'meaningful'. Relegating feedback to the relatively safe environment of a once-a-year performance review is not meaningful. In fact, such reviews often do more harm than good, turning into little more than the equivalent of a cold shower while managers list the perceived shortcomings of their team members. To make matters worse, annual reviews are often linked to salary reviews, so the employee takes in little of what the team leader is saying because they are too absorbed by wondering if they've made enough of an impact for a raise.

Feedback, difficult or otherwise, must be continuous. To be truly meaningful, it should be part of the daily and weekly routine. Some companies build it into their culture with regular events such as Feedback Friday. It might sound gimmicky, but it can be hugely effective. Alternatively, team leaders can ensure that they set time aside at the end of each project where the team as a whole can say how they thought they did and each individual can articulate their views on their own performance. It can be viewed as a built-in feedback charter for the team.

When feedback is easy and commonplace like this, everyone can walk away from sessions feeling energised, knowing what and how to improve. That includes the difficult stuff. Meaningful feedback becomes part of a learning culture, helping everyone to develop. It also:

- Creates a culture of trust and openness

- Helps engage employees by encouraging them to learn from their mistakes and improve their abilities

- Ensures clean lines of communication

- Energises the team and supports agility by enabling real-time performance adjustments to keep projects on track

- Acts as an incentive to stay put – employees are inspired by purpose-driven workplaces which prioritise their development

All of this starts from the top. Leaders play a key role in creating a culture of continuous feedback. Often, though, it's a struggle to put it into place because, inevitably, there will be times when difficult things need to be said. It's easy to fall into the trap of delaying *all* feedback because it is never quite the right time.

The key to resolving this is for leaders to learn how to handle difficult conversations in a way that produces a positive outcome. This means less pain for them and less pain for the person they talk to. It also paves the way for an environment where all feedback, good and bad, is regularly and effectively exchanged.

Shazia Ginai, Chief Growth Officer, Catalyx

There was a woman on the team, a real rock star in terms of performance. She started to study osteopathy part time and told me about it in confidence. At the time, I wasn't CEO, so she felt comfortable about the conversation.

When I was promoted to CEO, she felt uneasy. We sat down to talk about it and I said, 'Nothing changes.' I simply wanted to offer her the right amount of support she needed to do her job as well as her degree.

A while later, she came back to speak with me again. She needed to do a day a week in an osteopathy clinic as part of the course. She admitted that she had been really nervous about this conversation.

My first response was, 'How are you feeling? You must be so excited to start practising.' This was the emotionally intelligent way to begin.

When we pulled apart the logistics, the woman offered to do an extra hour or so each day to make up for the time away. This didn't seem like the best idea because she'd be exhausted. I suggested that she officially went down to four days and reduced her salary by 20%. We talked about how that would impact her household income and her personally.

By the end of the conversation, she had visibly changed because I had taken this emotional approach. She clearly felt a lot more at ease with the decision and realised she had options.

Emotional leadership is about opening up and helping others to understand there are choices for us all and, with a bit of creative thought, there is always a solution. It served me well too. Because I showed I care about her and what is important to her, she responded by showing me that she is dedicated to what we're doing. Her innovation and productivity rose hugely, even though she spent less time with us.

Preparation

Preparation and planning for difficult conversations is key, but it needs to be the right sort of preparation and planning. To return to Amy and her list, there were multiple reasons why this approach was all wrong. While it is crucial to plan, it is never good to write scripts like this.

What does count is to think about how you might feel and react on the day and to consider the same in the person you are speaking with. The carefully constructed list told me that Amy hadn't taken any time to reflect on the emotions that may be involved in this conversation. What, for example, was her direct report likely to be feeling? Equally importantly, how would *Amy* be feeling on the day?

Let's start with how you might feel if you are in the position of having to initiate and lead a difficult conversation. You will need to control yourself since this will be tricky emotionally, which may mean a change of mindset.

Anyone who goes into a conversation like this bracing themselves for a fight, as Amy did, will find that their emotions will rule them. It will be almost impossible to remain rational and clear-headed whatever path the conversation takes. If the person who called the meeting goes red in the face or has problems speaking or looks visibly stressed, the other party to that conversation is going to see that and take on that stress. In this situation, it is unlikely that either party will get the outcome they want.

Anticipating the likely emotions that could arise and understanding fully how we feel about the situation as well as the intentions for the conversation will help us to keep a clear head during the discussion. Spending some time beforehand thinking about how the other person feels and where they are coming from will also ensure that we approach the discussion in the right way. As leaders, we must think about how we are likely to react and our own potential trigger points.

I know, for example, that if I am facing an aggressive person who is open about how they feel, my tendency is to respond aggressively and sometimes explosively. Other people might clam up and withdraw in a similar situation. Knowing your own vulnerabilities and practising how you would like to come across during the conversation will give you an element of preparedness.

Emotional self-control can be quite hard to master, particularly in stressful situations. This is where many of the self-management techniques that we've already talked about are really important.

It may be a good idea to release any strong emotions prior to the discussion. I sometimes encourage my clients to talk or even vent about their feelings with a trusted friend or colleague ahead of the upcoming discussion. Venting in a safe space can be a powerful tool to release tension and prepare for that important discussion.

Practise some breathing exercises to get yourself into the zone ahead of the meeting. Get up-to-speed on actions that keep any anger at bay, such as anchoring. If during the meeting you sense your emotions rising, you'll then easily be able to reach for one of these self-control techniques to stop any uncomfortable thoughts derailing you.

Prepare yourself to take pauses in the discussion where necessary. The more calm and centred you are, the easier it will be to handle the conversation.

What, then, of the other side in this conversation? Most individuals don't take kindly to being told that they are failing or making mistakes, but there are ways that you can make it easier for them. Non-violent communication (NVC) skills are particularly useful here, so use words that emphasise observation without personal value judgements.

For example, rather than saying, 'You often don't listen when I am speaking', try something like, 'In our meeting today, I noticed that you were on your phone.' This is, after all, about their work performance, nothing else.

Similarly, difficult conversation should never include phrases like 'I'm disappointed' or 'It pains me to say this'. Phrases like this will only heighten the emotion around the occasion.

When you're planning for the meeting, think carefully about the person you will be speaking with. Different people like to receive feedback in different ways. What works well for some does not work for others. It's a great idea to take some time to discuss with the team how they like to receive feedback well ahead of the occasion when it needs to be given.

This doesn't have to be a big deal. Remember, individuals *want* feedback, so just pose the question, 'If I have to give you some constructive feedback, what will work best for you? Do you prefer to get straight into it or to have time to prepare?'

You may well discover that some individuals like to receive notice that there is going to be a difficult conversation so they can psychologically prepare themselves. In this case, it may help to send an email a day or so ahead of the conversation, saying, for example, 'Justin, I'd like to have a conversation about some of your work performance. Can we fix a chat for tomorrow?' With others, it is enough to say, 'Have you got five minutes? I'd like to have a chat with you.' The idea here is to respect the different human elements in a team.

Nobody takes unpleasant feedback easily. Understanding the preferences of individual members of the team is something that we learn as we develop our EQ. It all comes down to building connections and relationships with team members on an ongoing basis. This way, when you have feedback conversations, you know how to handle them.

Obviously, if there is a new person on the team and you haven't had time to properly get to know them yet, feedback is not something that you can prepare for. Ideally, though, it will be easy with established members of the team.

Finally, before the meeting, decide what it is you want to achieve. What is the outcome that you are looking for? You should, however, be prepared to adapt and let the discussion flow.

Getting started

It's the day of the difficult conversation. Except it isn't. Setting out with the mindset that you need to deliver something *difficult* has extremely negative connotations and will get everything off to a bad start. Think instead about all that you can do to have a constructive conversation and that will immediately get the endeavour off to a good start.

Think carefully about timing. Scheduling a feedback conversation in a brief gap between meetings is never a good idea. Both parties in this process need time and space to work with the emotions that are inevitably going to come up. The goal is, after all, that everyone feels at ease so the conversation is meaningful.

Likewise, avoid putting it in the diary for last thing on Friday afternoon. The other party will then have the entire weekend to ruminate on any uncomfortable aspects of the conversation. It is best to have these chats early in the week so they can come back for a further discussion once they've had a chance to digest what you've talked about.

The venue you choose for the conversation plays a part too. If, for example, there is a possibility that the person you're speaking with is suffering from stress, it may be best to meet outside of the office, perhaps even while taking a walk. A meeting room is not always conducive to extremely personal conversations. If the conversation *is* going to be held in the office, do it in a quiet place where there is little chance of interruption.

Working out the best opener is always a little nerve-wracking, however well you have prepared. One of the most effective ways to get through this is to ask for permission. You could say, 'May I share some feedback with you?' or 'May I tell you what I thought about your presentation last week?' or 'Would it be OK if I gave you some observations?'

Asking for permission encourages people to open up. It is also good to reassure them that everything said in the meeting is confidential. Keeping your tone neutral, go on to explain the reason for the chat. As you await the response, maintain an open mind. It may be that you have misinterpreted the intention of the team member or are overreacting and this situation will be more easy to resolve than you expected.

If you have done the groundwork well, the employee should speak freely about the issues under discussion. Use the active listening skills detailed in the previous chapter to show that you are interested in what is being said and want to understand the other person's point of view. Empathy is important, so show that what the employee is feeling matters and that you understand this is a delicate process.

While compassion and empathy are key skills in this situation, be wary of being overly sympathetic. Acknowledge that what each of you is saying may be difficult for the other person to hear, but do not stray over into responses such as 'I'm so sorry for you' or 'I know this is really hard for you.' There needs to be a balance between acknowledging that this is a tough conversation and that it has to be said. Once you sugar-coat the subject at hand, it blurs the conversation's true purpose.

The success of any feedback conversation depends upon a leader being fully present, bringing their whole self to the meeting and not rushing it. When you avoid working at breakneck speed to a tight timetable, you and the other party both have room to control your emotions and properly take in what is being said. You as leader can make sure that your interlocutor has understood the points being made and show genuine compassion and empathy.

Don't be afraid of silence. You must give adequate time for an individual to fully respond to what has been said. If it becomes obvious that the other person is struggling or can't seem to articulate what they are feeling, encourage them to pause and take a break from the conversation. This might be the moment to reassure them that you appreciate this conversation is delicate.

If during the conversation the emotion levels begin to rise significantly, pause the meeting. You can always come back to it again when you have both had time to calm down. The fight, flight or fright response, where the emotional part of the brain hijacks the rational part, may well impact both sides in this sort of meeting. Emotions will be heightened, so take time out if you feel the need. A pause for a cup of coffee or visit to the bathroom may be all that is required.

The conversation can end with an invitation to brainstorm possible solutions. This works well because it empowers the other person so they begin thinking about what they can do to change a situation. It is also a great opportunity for leaders to offer to mentor team members and help them to develop.

End the meeting by thanking the other person for being there, asking them how they feel about what has just happened and inviting them to add anything to the exchange. It is here that you find the balance between being clear and delivering what needs to be said, and making sure it's been understood while also checking in to see how the other person is feeling. This means paying attention to emotions at all times.

Done like this, feedback conversations can be really powerful rather than difficult. When a leader demonstrates that they can be a strong sounding board and shows that they care, it builds trust and strengthens their relationships with colleagues.

Once a culture of feedback is established in your organisation, even if your conversations involve delivering delicate feedback, members of the team will know they'll be listened to. This will in turn help them to be more willing to open up in the future. They may, of course, choose not to speak frankly. You can't force people to talk, but by trying and creating a safe emotional space, you can make a significant difference.

A conversation with someone suffering from chronic stress

There's a workshop we at HumanForce do with our clients which centres around having a conversation with a member of their team who may be suffering from chronic stress. We start it by giving them a scenario that may be found in any workplace today.

This scenario focuses on someone who has long been known as the star performer on the team, but in recent times, things have changed. We'll call him Oli here. The team leader, who we'll call Michelle, has noticed that Oli has become a bit late delivering his work and when it does come in, a number of mistakes are cropping up. At the moment, these are small, niggly mistakes, but they do add up.

Then there are rumours that Oli shouted at his assistant last week. When asked, the assistant says it's nothing, but Michelle suspects that they are covering up for Oli out of loyalty. They've been working together for ten years after all.

Now Michelle begins to think about it properly, she realises that Oli, who had always been the life and soul of the team, has stopped going out to lunch with his colleagues. It's been months since he's organised one of his much-liked bowling-night socials. Additionally, Oli looks tired. Really tired.

Each one of these behaviours is a sign that Oli is not doing well and may be suffering from chronic stress. He may even be close to burnout. Michelle is quite rightly worried about Oli and suspects that other members of the team are finding it difficult to work with him, but like his assistant, they are not saying anything out of long-held loyalty.

Michelle knows there needs to be a conversation and that it might be a delicate one. What, the Human-Force team asks at our workshops, would you do?

'Put yourselves in Michelle's shoes and tell us how you would handle it,' we say. The most common reaction is call in HR.

'This is an HR problem,' the participants in the workshop say. 'Someone from HR needs to get involved because Oli might react badly.'

This is entirely the wrong approach. Oli is a member of *Michelle*'s team. It's her role to care for him and understand what's going on. There shouldn't be a need to get HR involved straight off the bat. The only exception would be when there is tension because of a problem between Michelle and Oli.

If the need for delicate conversations among immediate team members is ignored or passed on to others to deal with, the entire working environment can rapidly become toxic because too many things are left unsaid. The plight of those employees who are suffering stress or close to burnout will go unnoticed, making their personal situation deteriorate, which will inevitably have an impact on the wider organisation too.

When it comes to having a conversation with someone who is likely to be suffering from chronic stress, many of the techniques to use are similar to the ones for having a delicate conversation. Similarly, this is not something that can be rushed. Give time for preparation and choose an appropriate neutral space to have the talk. The language you use is also key. Ask for permission to probe the issues and avoid being too personal or critical.

There are, however, some differences in approach. Since this is likely to be a stressful conversation, it is useful to quickly acknowledge the other person's worth and contribution to the team. This will help them to feel safe. In our example, as soon as Michelle says something like, 'Oli, you are a valued member of a team and I can see you are struggling,' he will immediately feel better about himself and be more willing to have a frank conversation.

If the employee expresses frustration about a chaotic work/life balance, agree that this can be difficult at times. You could express a little vulnerability by saying, 'I've been juggling my life too. It can be tough finding the balance between home and work.' Vulnerability like this can help people to open up, but as with sympathy and compassion, do not overdo it.

Above all, don't rush into trying to fix whatever problem they articulate. Despite all the careful planning, this will send everything off track within seconds of you opening the dialogue. Nearly every person in a position of leadership falls into this trap at some time or another; I know this first hand because it happens almost every time at HumanForce workshop chronic stress scenarios during coaching sessions. Those on the leadership side of our role play immediately jump in to try to fix the problem, instantly derailing the purpose of the chat.

It's easily done and, reading this, you may even recognise this response in yourself. Someone says they are feeling under stress or overwhelmed, or this or that isn't going well, and we rush to offer a solution. We say things like, 'Oh, I can remove this piece of work from your schedule to give you more time' or 'I can get another team to take over this project' or 'Why don't you take a couple of days off?'

It is laudable to try to help someone who expresses any sort of discomfort, but when we rush into solution mode, it means we are not really listening. If we don't listen to the whole story, we won't properly understand what's happening and won't be able to find the best way forward.

If you recognise that you are the type to rush towards solving issues, consciously take a step back. Remind yourself that you are there to listen and be curious. Instead of jumping in with ideas to fix the problem, prompt the other person to expand on it further by asking open-ended questions. Use the techniques we've already covered such as powerful questions, pausing, listening, reassuring and acknowledging. Keep an eye on how the other person is taking the discussion by regularly checking in with them.

You may be able to offer help or suggest solutions at the end of the conversation, but this should not be the focus of this type of meeting. There could be countless reasons behind what is impacting this employee. What you want to do here is listen and understand what's going on. This is where you become an emotional detective to find out what is causing the stress and see how badly it is affecting them. Could there be something that you don't know about? Is it worse than you imagined? Are they close to burnout? These are all things that a team leader needs to know.

Leaders don't always need to present solutions. Sometimes they just need to be in listening mode and that's enough. Solutions can be the subject of another conversation at a later date, when all parties have had time to properly digest the initial conversation.

In Oli's case, it may be that HR does eventually need to become involved, but what is most important is that the conversation has been initiated by the team leader, which will, in turn, be invaluable in shaping a solution if needed. Without trying to offer an immediate fix, help the other person to see that there are always ways out of any problems. Emphasise that there are solutions and the two of you can work on them together going forward.

Dealing with conflict

Conflict at work is normal. It doesn't matter what kind of company you lead or the sector it operates in, some sort of conflict between colleagues is inevitable. This is particularly so nowadays with diverse multicultural teams working in a range of settings from in the office to hybrid, all of which opens the door for the occasional misunderstanding or for things to get lost in communication. Similarly, in a rapidly changing world, uncertainty fuels conflict.

Conflict occurs at every level of an organisation too, whether it is a clash between two team members over how a task is done or between directors over differing goals and values. Poor leadership and a lack of clarity can also create flashpoints.

During the COVID-19 period, I noticed that there were a lot more conflicts among the workplace teams I work with than there had been prior to the pandemic because stress is always a significant trigger. However, many of the people involved were reluctant to acknowledge it. There is a certain taboo around conflict. If it is discussed at all, it is frequently quickly passed on to HR.

'Isn't it an HR role to deal with conflict resolution?' people ask. 'It's not something that needs to be dealt with by everybody.' The opposite is, in fact, true. Conflict in the workplace is something we all need to acknowledge and deal with.

Conflict is a necessary part of our daily work. If team leaders learn how to deal with it, they will build strong bonds among the humanforce. Managing conflict well also plays a significant role in helping to reap all the benefits from diverse multicultural teams. While any sort of conflict can be uncomfortable, it can also be a rich source of creativity and innovation. When leaders deal with it effectively, it can be a powerful driver of change. Manage it badly, though, and it can derail projects, damage relationships internally and externally, and harm productivity.

When we feel strongly about something, it is a sure-fire indicator that something is wrong or something that we really believe in is under threat, or perhaps our boundaries have been violated. Each of these scenarios provokes strong emotions. The main emotions involved in conflict are anger, anxiety and fear, all energy-draining emotions, which is perhaps why many leaders shy away from tackling conflicts, even if they've been rumbling on for some time. They may prefer to keep at a distance from the disagreement because they are frightened of what might happen when they address unpleasant emotions. Because of this, they will miss the opportunity to resolve the conflict.

Successful conflict resolution relies on leaders anticipating situations that might explode rather than ignoring them or pushing them to one side. Left unchecked or dealt with in a mediocre way, strong emotions will simmer beneath the surface until they eventually burst forth in a potentially catastrophic way.

There are different stages of conflict, ranging from people being mildly irritated by something someone has said or done to being on the brink of a full-blown rage, and each one fuels a range of emotions. The emotion of fear plays a big role, even at the mildest level, and this fear can be a hurdle to sorting out the issue in question.

Another emotion in play could be anxiety that addressing the conflict could cause long-term harm to a relationship with a colleague or may even harm one's own reputation. We could potentially make matters worse and increase the level of conflict. Alternatively, as leadership expert Annie McKee suggests, conflict makes us feel worried and nervous because we sense we are going to have to give something up, whether it is our true point of view or the way we are accustomed to doing something, or even some of our power.

What is interesting to note is this shows that conflict is rarely about what *actually happened*, but more about the meaning people attach to the event. Team leaders need to approach conflict from this viewpoint. They need to show the people around them that they have listened, care about what has been said and have their best interests at heart.

If a conflict does arise, it's useful to organise a discussion between the affected colleagues at the earliest opportunity to resolve it. Leaders should prepare well in advance of such a discussion to anticipate what emotions might arise to make sure they approach the conversation in the right way. EQ plays a key role here since it is crucial to understand what drives each team member involved. This will help them deal with some of their anxiety and in turn shape their approach to the conversation.

As I shared earlier, I know, for example, that when I am facing an aggressive person, my natural tendency is to respond aggressively and this would not be appropriate. Alternatively, some people will clam up completely in such a situation and may need to be led through the conversation.

As leader, you also need to pause to check that you yourself are in the right emotional frame of mind. Is this the right time to have this conversation or do you need to take a walk first or have a mindful moment? If you are not mindful of this, your own emotions can seep out during difficult conversations.

In all cases, the team members in the midst of the conflict will be nervous about the forthcoming conversation. Put processes in place so that all the issues can be aired, everybody knows what their roles are and each person ends the meeting feeling that others have heard where they are coming from. Everyone involved should be given ample opportunity to speak frankly about what is important to them.

Being in the present is another crucial skill for leaders involved in such discussions. Use active listening skills to demonstrate that you are properly registering what is being said and give the team members concerned your full attention. Body language is important, which means facing the individuals involved, maintaining eye contact and not getting distracted.

What happens, though, when you are in the midst of a situation that is becoming conflictual or if the conflict suddenly arises and you do not have time to prepare? As we have seen, when stress occurs, we go into our fight or flight response as we try to protect or defend ourselves. It is not always ideal to be defensive in a conflict situation, so it is important to learn how to handle that fight or flight response.

This is where emotional self-regulation tools are really useful. Whether it's taking a pause or excusing yourself from the room, do what you can to work with your emotions so they don't overwhelm you. Concentrating on your breathing and using the anchoring techniques are options to help you respond rather than react. If the situation does get too heated, it might be wise to walk away and postpone talking about it until a later stage.

One of the main actions that leaders can take to reduce the fallout from disagreements and stop them from negatively impacting their teams is to show conflict as a positive thing. This opens space for an honest dialogue where members of the team can voice their feelings and opinions respectfully and without aggression.

In some instances, conflicts are quite easy to resolve. Take for example a situation where two people are asked to work together on a project. Right at the start of the process, one of them is late delivering their side, which will upset the other person involved.

While it might be easy to rush to judgement, a better solution for the upset person is to askA why the work was delivered late. Did their partner in the project forget? Is it simply their more relaxed working style? Are there any measures that they can put in place to help them work together more effectively? It is much better to get an agreement in place early on rather than saying nothing at all, which inevitably leads to simmering resentment between colleagues.

We can all let small incidents like this slide, but if they are allowed to fester, they get compounded. Each time something doesn't go as planned, it builds upon the bad feelings from the previous time. Many conflicts are the result of emotions that have been allowed to build up over periods of time.

Leaders need to create an environment where everyone feels able to check in with colleagues to make sure situations like this do not go unresolved. In this safe space, people can feel free to talk and vent any emotions. If, however, the conflict does escalate, leaders may need to intervene more proactively while remaining calm to be able to see the situation clearly. This means keeping their eyes open so they are aware of what's going on within the team and can tune into the emotions of the group.

Again, many of the tools we have already covered are useful here, such as showing empathy and active listening. Leaders listen, and then acknowledge and reframe what they have heard to show they understand, because validation is important here. Those who are deep into a conflict situation want to know their concerns have been heard.

The goal is to de-escalate the problem and to come up with a solution that is acceptable to all. It really helps if the leader has already laid the groundwork and the team believes that their boss cares about them and trusts their judgement.

Summary

Leaders may shy away from delicate conversations for a multitude of reasons, but the factor that unites this reluctance to act is emotions. More specifically, it's energy-draining emotions such as fear, sadness, shame or disappointment. Since these are emotions we can't avoid when we're having delicate conversations, we distance ourselves from the whole idea.

Does this matter? Yes, it does. It is your job as a leader to develop your team members. Sometimes, that means having delicate conversations about under-performance or poor behaviour, otherwise they won't learn from their mistakes or see areas where they can improve and be the best they can be. This is a key reason why people actively *want* this kind of feedback.

In this chapter, we have looked closely at the so-called 'difficult' conversations and examined how to make sure they are an integral part of your company culture. We've also looked at how to handle it if conflict does arise among the individuals on your team, which inevitably it will at some point.

EIGHT
Gender And Emotions

Clara's career trajectory was exceptional. In eight years with her company, she had been promoted five times. It was hardly surprising because she brought an unprecedented energy to each role, achieving top results every time. Her performance encouraged her team to push themselves too.

Yet, as Clara moved up within the company, she became increasingly disaffected and disengaged. Her senior colleagues would repeatedly tell her she was too emotional. The higher she went in the company, the more she was encouraged to tone it down. When I spoke with Clara, she was at her wits' end and wondering if the best course of action was to move on.

To Clara, being animated and passionate was part of her culture. She had been brought up in Spain in a large household where it was quite common for everyone to speak at once and express their views with passion. Somehow, though, everyone got their point across.

'When I give presentations, I can tell my colleagues are looking at me and thinking I am too excited or becoming too animated,' she told me. 'But why is being excited about an idea a *bad* thing? I feel like I am not being taken seriously.'

Clara's experience is not simply down to a gulf between cultural understandings. I have spoken to countless other women whose stories are not dissimilar from Clara's. Certainly, when I deliver emotional agility training to female leaders each year, it's a common theme.

Women often find the subject of how to deal with emotions in the workplace really tricky. So many of them have experienced moments where they get excited or demonstrate they feel strongly about something, only to be told to calm down or to speak in a more rational manner. Their male colleagues seem keener on admonishing them for being too emotional than actually listening to what it is they are so passionate about. As a result, no one is sure whether they can be their true selves at work. If they feel strongly about something, should they dampen down how they feel?

In one study of more than 1,000 360-degree peer-reviewed feedback reports on female executives, their male colleagues made notes like 'she was too hyped up' or 'too emotional'.[1] Women executives commenting on the same incidents that provoked these dismissive reviews said their female colleagues were simply putting forward their opinions, albeit passionately. What makes it more frustrating is some women feel compelled to speak with passion and force to compensate for not being listened to by their male colleagues. They feel they are not taken seriously by men when they communicate quietly and evenly.

Ironically, though, this passion may lead men to take women even *less* seriously, because passion and emotion is not the norm they are used to when they communicate with each other professionally. As a result, women's opinions do not land, at least not as intended. The male colleagues who accused their female counterparts of being too emotional also commented that unchecked emotion made any ideas less convincing to them and compromised the credibility of the person forwarding them.

Assumptions about women based on their emotional responses are present in every aspect of the working world. Women will find themselves pushed towards roles in keeping with the (possibly 'acceptable') types of emotions that they are more prone to display than men, such as kindness, compassion and humanity. Thus, they are frequently put in charge of health and wellbeing initiatives or HR roles where they deal with sensitive issues or in setting up community activities.

To add to the general confusion about which 'self' women should bring to work, there are some double standards to be thrown into the mix. Any woman who aspires to a leadership position has to immediately drop the kind and gentle persona and become tough, authoritative and prepared to stand her ground.

Christiane Bisanzio, Thought Leader, Diversity and Inclusion

Sometimes, women feel like they can't win. It's a glass-half-empty statement, but it is true.

One of the big issues is the complete gulf in understanding between different styles of leading. Take strategic thinking. All leaders, male and female, are required to be top-notch strategic thinkers. Some men point the finger and say women can't be good strategic thinkers because they take too long, yet the reason why women don't simply whip out a strategic plan is because they like to take the time to listen. The female leader doesn't spend her time speaking over her colleagues and rushing towards a conclusion because she really wants to hear their views.

Men and women are simply different. We should celebrate that as a positive and take away the illogical arguments focused on something entirely irrelevant.

Hardly surprisingly, thanks to this prejudice and misinterpretation, women feel like they are constantly walking a tightrope. Are they too kind? If they are, they're seen as a pushover. Yet, if they're too authoritative and always stand their ground, they're dismissed as a bitch.

How emotionally different are men and women?

STUDY: Little evidence for sex or ovarian hormone influences on affective variability[2]

Are women really more emotional than men? Do their emotions fluctuate wildly throughout their monthly cycle, as the gender stereotype will have us believe? These are questions that a group of researchers from the University of Michigan set out to answer.

For seventy-five days, the team followed 142 men and women to observe and log their regular emotions. The women in the group included those with 'natural' menstrual cycles and those who were using three different types of oral contraceptive. At the end of the study, the researchers concluded that the men's emotions fluctuated just as much as those of the women in the group. Emotional highs and lows are due to many influences, the study said, not only hormones.

Researchers say there are some differences in the way men and women react from an emotional perspective because of differences in our brains.[3] A woman has a greater blood flow in the cingulate gyrus, the part of the brain that's involved in processing emotions. This leads to more intense emotional reactions and stronger emotional memories than men experience.

There is also more wiring in the areas of a woman's brain that are concerned with social cognition and verbal communication. Thus, women are generally more empathetic with a better sense of what is going on around them and they're able to articulate it more richly than men. Men have less connectivity than women between their emotional centres and their emotions and memories, so are not as effective as communicators. This may be why they have less interest in intense conversations.

While men and women are, indeed, wired differently, what is less certain is whether we were born like this. Brain connections change thanks to our experiences and learned behaviour. When the same signal is processed again and again, the neural networks get stronger. We know girls and boys are treated differently from the moment they are born. Many boys are raised to hide their emotions while society says it is more acceptable for girls to show their feelings (but not too much in the workplace, girls).

Regardless of whether women have become hardwired to be more emotional than men, there are some emotional responses, such as crying, that can be difficult to control. Women have 60% more prolactin than the average male. This is the reproductive hormone that stimulates the production of milk following childbirth. Tears brought on by emotion are extremely high in prolactin, which may explain why women's tears flow more easily than a man's.

Similarly, men may cry less than women because testosterone levels inhibit crying. Women tend to cry for a range of reasons over and above being sad.

They will cry when they are angry or frustrated, for example. One study found that women cry on average 5.3 times a month, compared to an average of 1.3 times per month for men.[4]

Men, on the other hand, veer towards physical expressions of strong emotion, particularly when they are cross, such as banging their fists on the table.[5] Alternatively, they will shout. Men are almost twice as likely to start shouting than women (43% versus 26%), with triggers such as their 'ideas not being heard' or 'being criticised' being cited. They are three times as likely to get emotional if a project goes over budget, misses a deadline or gets cancelled. It is also men who are more likely than women to vote with their feet and quit a job when their emotions boil over (20% versus 11%).

To summarise, men are more likely to express powerful emotions such as anger and pride, partly because they have been conditioned not to display any feelings other than anger, whereas women err more towards the sadness, guilt and shame side. So yes, both men and women have masculine and feminine energies, but we express our emotions and respond differently.

The real problem lies in our response

Often, it is not emotions that are the issue; it is the way we react to them in the workplace. Organisations frequently build their cultures around entirely unrealistic expectations on how men and women should behave, even though many of these behaviours have roots in outdated traditions that go far back in time.

The widely held notion that 'real' men work until the point of exhaustion can be traced to the seventeenth-century Protestant ethic, in which hard work was seen as a calling to serve God and society. This idea has endured so that even today, working long hours is believed to be a sign of loyalty and anyone who complains or is simply not able to keep up the pace is 'not one of us'. Unrealistic expectations about the 'right' way to behave abound and build a toxic culture where those who don't conform are singled out.

What employers should be doing is putting policies and practices in place that allow people to properly express themselves and not be so tightly tied into a one-size-fits-all culture. As it is, many team members find themselves second guessing how best to behave, what emotions they can and can't show and to what extent. This in turn perpetuates the toxic culture because individuals will be hard on their colleagues who don't act in a certain way.

Take crying at work as an example. A large percentage of workers frown upon the practice, saying no, crying at work is not acceptable, and often colleagues can be harder on their co-workers about this subject than executives. Among employees, 32% said it was never OK to shed tears at work compared to 26% of executives, although this apparently more forgiving side to senior teams is somewhat undermined by the fact 44% of chief finance officers believe crying too often can undermine career prospects.[6]

How about anger, then? How acceptable is it to show anger during the working day? More than half of employees (52%) have lost their temper in the workplace,[7] but after years of social conditioning, it is apparently more acceptable for men to be angry than their female colleagues. Research has shown that expressions of anger are seen as a sign of competence and high status for men.[8]

Anger and aggression are subconscious reactions to suppressing any sign of weakness and maintaining or even growing a place in the pecking order. It's a universal shorthand, too; male job applicants who express anger are more likely to be hired than those who express sadness. They are also subsequently given more power and autonomy in their jobs. However, when women express anger, it can decrease rather than increase their status and perceived competence. Anger in men is viewed as a response to an outside circumstance with the understanding being that they were provoked. In women, displays of anger are viewed as an intrinsic trait: she is an *angry person*.

So much of the workplace perception of emotion is unfair and confusing. In nearly all cases, it puts everyone at a disadvantage.

Let's start with the impact upon women. It seems ironic that one of the reasons women are, or are seen to be, more emotional than men at work is because they take their role more personally. Research shows that women are more likely than men to want their work to have meaning and purpose.[9] Therefore, it's logical that they may respond more passionately and emotionally in any given work situation. They are simply more attached and emotionally engaged. The irony is, as the following study shows, this engagement can actually be harming women's long-term career prospects.

STUDY: Gender and emotions at work: organisational rank has greater emotional benefits for men than women[10]

How much do negative perceptions of showing 'too much' emotion impact a woman's career prospects? Quite a lot, according to a survey which says the impact is akin to women running with leaded shoes.

Research using data from 14,615 adult male and female workers found that, at the lowest level of employment, women reported feeling significantly more respected than men. However, as the careers of both genders climbed within an organisation, this position reversed. Women experienced more negative and fewer positive feelings. Since emotions influence job performance, decision making, creativity, conflict resolution and leadership effectiveness, this puts women at a disadvantage in attaining the next promotion. Women who feel overwhelmed, stressed, less respected and less confident than men find it hard to break through the glass ceiling, researchers note.

The pressure to always be strong, powerful and in control takes its toll upon men. Repressing strong emotions has a detrimental impact on mental health, leading to risk taking, substance abuse and depression. There is no doubt that it also leads to the disproportionately high suicide rate in men.

Suicide is the leading cause of death for men under fifty. Of the average 6,000 people who take their own lives each year, three quarters are men.[11] Often, no one knows that a male colleague is struggling until it is too late because men have fewer friendship groups than their female peers and are much less likely to open up about what they are experiencing.

How leaders can redress the balance . . .

Perhaps the underlying issue that has got us to the situation we are in today is that the norms and expectations in the world of work have been set by men to reflect the way they do things. Ideally, the place we need to get to is one where a woman's way of doing things with a little added emotion and passion is viewed as just as normal and valid. We are, however, a little way from that day. In the meantime, this gender disparity around emotions at work needs to be tackled from all sides: from an organisational viewpoint, by individual leaders and by team members themselves, both male and female.

Let's begin with organisations as a whole. Businesses everywhere need to redress the balance on emotions. As previously noted, too many organisations continue to stick rigidly to the cultural norms where both men and women are, on an equal basis, supposed to push forward and not show any emotions.

This is particularly so in certain sectors, such as the finance and legal industries, which have historically valued team members remaining stoic at all times and putting in long hours without complaint. There is little recognition or understanding of the place of emotions in the daily workload. This allows misconceptions around emotions to thrive in the workplace, putting both male and female members of the team at a disadvantage and contributing to their feeling of exclusion.

Organisation leaders need to break down this myth and make it clear that stereotypes where men are tough and women are soft are no longer valid. There is plenty of evidence to show that both genders are equally committed to balancing work and family life,[12] so it makes perfect sense to offer the same support and opportunities for flexible working to men and women, especially if they have responsibilities as carers for a young family or an elderly parent. This should be ingrained in company policy.

Leaders have a crucial role to play in bringing the disparity between how men and women are treated and regarded in the workplace into the open so everyone is better informed. They need to make a public acknowledgement that men and women do function differently, but when women are more emotional, it doesn't mean that they are not competent or leadership material. They simply display their feelings in a different way.

Likewise, leaders need to model the way in breaking down the stereotype that men need to be strong and assertive, and women kind and gentle. This is an essential step when we're working towards getting greater numbers of women into leadership roles – something that is long overdue. Leadership requires strength and assertiveness and that can come from a woman as well as a man. Everyone in an organisation needs to accept that women leaders won't be sweet and nice, because leaders can't be like that all the time.

One area that needs particular attention is around potentially divisive situations such as parental leave when a baby is born. Paternity leave is now mandated by law in many countries, but often men are reluctant to take advantage of the offer because they are afraid of how it will look to colleagues. The undercurrent of bias against caregivers, aka working mothers,[13] has long been known, manifesting itself in a variety of ways from lower performance evaluation to fewer opportunities for progression than others enjoy. Ergo, taking paternity leave may impact a man's career too, or so the thinking goes.

There is a double bind here for men. As well as worrying about their career prospects if they take time off to spend with their newborn, they will also be anxious about missing out on key moments with their young family. Younger people today are much more likely than older generations to want to share parenting roles and key moments such as putting children to bed.

In all cases, there needs to be an inclusive discussion to lay out expectations and to give assurances. Part of this process is to make an agreement about what's acceptable in a particular workplace and what's not. Again, leaders need to model the way.

In the case of parental leave, for example, leaders should not simply communicate that the option is available. They should actively encourage everyone to take their full allocation. To achieve this massive shift in behaviour, the new model will need to be almost over-communicated, so everyone on the ground believes that this is what leadership truly wants.

Men and women need to be comfortable about the fact that any emotional response won't be held against them. It might not be appropriate to give everyone the green light to cry at their desks whenever they like (I will talk more about this in the next section) or to shout at colleagues, but if a woman is feeling vulnerable, there could be some flexibility. She could, for example, be given some time off or allowed to work from home that day.

Meanwhile, men can be helped to understand that a little vulnerability is OK in certain circumstances. Team leaders can signal it is alright to talk about emotions by using many of the techniques already flagged here, such as sharing their own vulnerabilities and offering safe spaces where men can open up about their own experiences.

. . . and how team members can help themselves

We have looked at multiple strategies to help regulate strong emotions, from breathing through complex situations to practising mindfulness on a daily basis. These are all valid techniques, but are there any gender-specific techniques that will help?

Let's begin with men. Male employees need to learn how to speak out. They are battling with many of the same issues that working women have faced for years, namely balancing work and home responsibilities. They may be in a highly demanding job where their bosses are expecting them to complete a task *now*, but they may also have agreed to do the school pick up that day. Who do they let down? Their manager or their partner?

The answer is neither. Instead, men have to accept that they will need to share their concerns. It is not showing weakness to hold an open, honest conversation at work where expectations can be shifted. The work can still get done that day, but perhaps after all the domestic chores are complete.

The starting point here is for men to fully accept we all have emotions and it is hugely damaging to our mental and physical health to pretend they are not there.

Elliott Rae, Founder and Editor-in-Chief, Music.Football. Fatherhood.

A football game is a most emotional experience and probably the only one where men ever feel safe to express any major emotions. When you see men at a football game, they express *all* the emotions: they are angry, happy or sad. When their team loses, it is perfectly acceptable for a grown man to cry for an hour after the game has finished. If they win, it is fine for them to jump up and down and hug and kiss their friends. It's all normal and respected.

A lot of men use the game on a Saturday to vent all of the emotions they've been bottling all week. They are not just angry, happy or sad because of a bunch of men kicking a ball around a pitch; they're emotional about what has happened before. What they really need is to acknowledge that emotions have a role to play every day and to actively work with them.

For men, the best thing they can do is to get to know themselves, how they think and what they really want out of life. It is easy to get assimilated into a high-pressure working environment and get carried along by it, but if you know who you are and what you want, it makes it simple to change course. It is hugely important to find a strong friendship group and surround yourself with other men who have similar values. We all need strong allies when we want to make big changes.

What about women, then? What can they do if they find themselves constantly suppressing tears or toning down their passion for projects? It does, after all, mean they are not really bringing their full selves to work.

Many of the female leaders I interviewed for this book say they always insist on being themselves at work. If they find themselves in a workplace where they can't properly express emotions, then they will take steps to leave because the environment will be just too toxic. They don't want to be somewhere that is costly for their health and wellbeing.

This was, in part, the advice I gave to Clara, the talented lady this chapter opened with. I advised her under no circumstances to lose her passion for the role, but when she had a meeting with her team leaders, she should prepare well in advance and be aware of the people who would be in a room with her. A little bit of anticipation might help, but she nevertheless needed to bring her true self to the meeting.

Hajar El Haddaoui, who we heard from earlier, gives us a good example of how she handled an awkward situation at work.

Hajar El Haddaoui, Senior Director, Executive Board Member

I was in a board meeting with my peers and we were discussing the budget, which is a very pragmatic and rational topic. When I gave my feedback, one of my colleagues said, 'Oh, you are too emotional today.' I said nothing and reflected on the comment, which I felt was unacceptable.

> At the next meeting, this person got rather angry and frustrated. I pointed out that he was rather emotional and asked him what was going on. It was a wake-up call for him. He apologised and said that he was not aware of the impact of his previous comment.
>
> I will not adapt my style.

I hear stories like this time and time again. Senior female leaders tell me that they do not want to adapt during meetings, but would rather build a safe space within the C-Suite where discrimination and bias are not accepted. Women need to challenge and drive change. Stereotypes must be tackled from the top.

What does this mean in practice? To remain authentic and to be heard during meetings, what can women do? What are some of the tactics that they might put in place to give them a fair share of the voice?

> **Gill Whitty-Collins, Author, Non-Executive Director, Consultant and Executive Coach**
>
> Meetings can be difficult for many women because they're usually dominated by their male colleagues who feel more comfortable and confident in the culture. Women frequently find themselves with a lower share of voice and are significantly more likely to be interrupted than when men are speaking. (Men interrupt 33% more often when they speak with a woman than they do when speaking to another man.)[14]

> Often, when women do get to speak, their points
> of view are not listened to or heard. Many women
> have expressed frustration that they've made a valid
> point in a meeting only for it to be ignored, then later
> repeated by a man and celebrated by the group as if it
> was the first time that they had ever heard it.

Gill goes on to add that there are a few steps that can be taken that will vastly redress the balance in meetings. The first one is to request that each meeting has a proper chairperson to ensure that everyone gets a fair chance to speak without interruption. Secondly, women must not try to emulate the way their male colleagues behave in meetings, but contribute authentically from the foundations of their strengths and expertise, what she calls their 'confident core'.

'When we speak from here,' Gill adds, 'people can feel our authentic confidence and they listen. Our share of voice or speaking time is not important.'

If interrupted or talked over, women can say something like, 'Allow me to finish my thoughts, then I'll hand the floor over to you.' This calm response takes the power back from the person doing the interrupting.

Similarly, if someone sees another woman getting interrupted, the most powerful thing they can do is to support them by saying something like, 'You were interrupted, but I'd like to hear the rest of your point.' This role models the right meeting behaviour and also, as a bonus, makes the person who interrupted look and feel foolish, which may (hopefully) put them off from doing it again in the future.

Finally, what is the recommendation when it comes to crying in the workplace? Is it OK to cry? This is a difficult one with many different moving parts. As I described earlier, crying is part of a woman's authentic self and they do it so much more easily than men, although it does seem acceptable for male sports stars to shed the odd tear.

Crying doesn't show that we're weak; it just shows that something is important to us. Telling a woman to suppress this natural act could be seen as reinforcing the culture and norms that support male dominance. After all, if the goal is that we bring our whole self to work, women should let the tears flow if they need to.

On the other hand, it is hard to imagine a world where crying openly is seen as positive or even neutral in the workplace. As the statistics show, it is still widely frowned upon. Perhaps if women had made up 50% of the workforce from the beginning of time, this natural behaviour would be a valid part of professional life. Who knows, perhaps one day that will happen, but for now, while crying in the workplace is read as undermining a woman's credibility, it would be unwise to add any more ammunition against women. Therefore, my recommendation would be for women to hold back their tears until they can get to the privacy of the loos.

Summary

Women often find the subject of how to deal with emotions in the workplace tricky. So many of them have experienced moments where they get excited or demonstrate they feel strongly about something, only to be told to calm down or to speak in a more rational manner. Women may find themselves pushed towards roles in keeping with the types of emotions that they are more prone to display than men, such as kindness, compassion and humanity.

To add to the general confusion about which 'self' women should bring to work, there are some double standards at play. Any woman who aspires to a leadership position has to drop the kind and gentle persona and become tough, authoritative and prepared to stand her ground. Men have their own challenges around the expression of emotion at work and just like women are expected to display certain emotions such as anger and pride. Organisation leaders need to make it clear that stereotypes where men are tough and women are soft are no longer valid. Leaders can encourage inclusive discussions to lay out expectations and give assurances around showing emotion. Part of this process is to make an agreement about what's acceptable in a particular workplace and what's not.

PART THREE
THE EMOTIONAL CULTURE

NINE

Building A Positive Emotional Culture

We have, or so most organisation leaders like to think, come a long way from the high-pressure, high-stress workplaces depicted in countless movies from *The Devil Wears Prada* to *Wall Street*. The myth that a cut-throat environment somehow cajoles employees into giving their best possible performance (and perhaps even a little bit more) has now been thoroughly debunked.

It is widely accepted that the main outcome from such unrelenting pressure is a rapidly rising rate of disconnection, disengagement and even serious illness from burnout. As a result, unprecedented resources are being invested into initiatives to create a positive employee experience. Nine in ten organisations around the world now offer some sort of wellness programme.[1] Much is made of 'beautiful' workspaces, boasting amenities from breakout pods to fully equipped gyms, plus additional perks such as well-being days, all designed to inspire employees, helping them to relax and bring their best selves to work.

As laudable as these efforts to prioritise employee health and wellbeing are, they are often not as holistic as they sound. I'll give you a great example.

My work brings me into contact with numerous companies in Switzerland. This country has been voted as the best all-round destination for a career abroad, thanks to a winning combination of excellent earning prospects, strong job security, a stunning working environment and an enjoyable work culture.[2] When I speak with teams on the ground, though, a slightly different picture sometimes emerges.

Yes, they say, their employers have built a fantastic gym, stocked with all the latest kit, but their workload is so heavy, they rarely have time for a workout. As for that stunning lake view easily visible through the gleaming floor-to-ceiling windows, they barely get a chance to look up and notice their surroundings. The feeling of always being on call, together with an unreasonable workload, low autonomy and a lack of social support, cancels out many of the positives of the wellness initiatives.

This is not to single out Switzerland. After all, as the high approval ratings suggest, Swiss employers are without a doubt heading in the right direction. However, they are still falling short. What organisations there and, indeed, around the world need to offer is a rounded *human-orientated* experience or, more specifically, a positive emotional culture.

When the word 'culture' is used, most people immediately think about *cognitive* culture, in other words 'how things get done around here'. Cognitive culture describes the shared intellectual values, norms and assumptions that many organisations document in a bid to help their teams work together more effectively. It sets out a company-wide understanding of how much an individual firm values being customer-focused or innovative or team orientated or competitive, and that sets the tone.

While cognitive culture is important, it only tells half the story. The other side to that story is *emotional* culture. Emotional culture is more focused on feelings, moods and attitudes.

Every organisation in every sector around the world has an emotional culture because they are all staffed by human beings, and we are emotional. To return to the perspective of how things get done around here, when a business's leaders recognise its emotional culture, it shows that they are paying attention to how employees are or should be feeling. Business leaders who really want to get the best out of their employees need to go further than simply satisfying their basic human needs with smart offices and good working conditions. They need to build a strong emotional culture which recognises their *human* qualities as well.

Business leaders who overlook emotional culture are setting themselves up for a fall. They are glossing over a vital part of what makes individuals and, indeed, the entire organisation tick. I know from my own experience that all the times I have resigned and left a workplace, it's been because my manager failed to engage me or because I didn't feel trusted and valued or that my human needs had been respected. It was these emotional reactions that were the deciding factors when I chose to move on, rather than the quality or scope of the work. The presence of a gym, or not, had no bearing whatsoever on my decision.

Employee engagement = emotional commitment to an organisation

In all the acres of print and endless discussions about the war for talent, there is always a common thread: employee engagement. Keeping employees engaged is an increasing priority for companies for a multitude of reasons. They tend to stick around for a lot longer than those employees who are not engaged, which is a significant benefit when it can cost an organisation more than 30% of an annual salary to replace each person who resigns.[3] Engaged employees outperform their peers by 140% in earnings per share,[4] not to mention having a significantly positive impact on productivity. They are also more innovative, better with customers and more empathetic towards co-workers.

Conversely, when employees feel undervalued, unsupported or insecure in their jobs, they become stressed and disengaged. It's estimated that 650 million workdays are lost each year worldwide due to stress, depression and anxiety.[5]

What does 'engaged' really mean in this context? Like many corporate buzzwords, the true meaning often gets lost in the repetition. Yes, we know it's not something that can simply be ordered up just like that. It's voluntary and it's individual, so how can we define employee engagement?

Opinions vary. Gallup cites engaged employees as those who are 'involved in, enthusiastic about and committed to their work and workplace'. Management consultant Aon Hewitt, on the other hand, defines it as 'the level of an employee's psychological investment in their organisation'.[6] To me, the closest definition is the one offered by HR software provider Quantum Workplace. It says employee engagement is 'the mental and emotional connection employees feel toward their places of work'.[7]

Our level of engagement in the workplace is therefore defined by the depth of our emotional commitment.[8] Without a doubt, workplaces where individuals feel comfortable expressing their feelings are productive, creative, collaborative and innovative.

What is the emotional culture in your office right now? Unlike cognitive culture, the emotional culture that currently exists might at first glance seem invisible or certainly quite subtle, but it's there if you look hard enough and, rest assured, everyone who works with you will be aware of it, if only subconsciously. Even brand-new employees will pick up on the clues straight away.

In fact, the process that individuals go through from their first day in a new job is known as an emotional learning cycle.[9] Here, what happens to them in their first few weeks and the way it is dealt with will establish their understanding of the cultural norms and influence many of their subsequent emotional reactions and how they handle them.

Say, for example, this new employee experiences bullying or witnesses one of their colleagues being belittled. If the event is well-handled by their team leader, it will shape their future view of what is and isn't OK. If the incident is not dealt with properly or quietly brushed under the carpet, it will be a red flag. The new employee will understand that kindness and compassion are not priorities in this firm and only the toughest survive. This will, in turn, have an impact on the coping strategies that they adopt.

Other signs of a positive emotional culture can be found in the way people greet each other, conduct meetings, discuss issues and communicate online. Obviously, it's a good sign if the communication system between team members is two-way and employee-centred, emphasising listening, reciprocity and feedback, and valuing employees' voices and inputs. Likewise, when leaders at different levels communicate in a responsive, friendly, warm, compassionate and caring manner, their teams are more likely to follow their lead. A culture of love, joy, pride and gratitude is likely to develop.

STUDY: Is love all you need? The effects of emotional culture, suppression and work-family conflict on firefighter risk-taking and health[10]

A study by professors Olivia O'Neill and Nancy Rothbard of firefighters stationed in major metropolitan areas found that units that were defined by two emotions, joviality and companionate love, were better able to cope with the stresses of the job. The firefighters also more effectively managed the family conflicts that arose from the intense and unpredictable jobs that they had. Those firefighters who operated in stations where the suppression of emotions was encouraged experienced high work/family conflict and reported more risk-taking behaviour outside of work.

Employees thrive in cultures that foster joy, love and fun. These are the emotions that influence an employee's creativity, decision making, quality of work and commitment. They are what will bind the organisation together, build engagement and, in turn, have a huge impact on performance.

Further research done by Olivia O'Neill together with business theorist Sigal Barsade found that the focus on creating positive emotional cultures often gives organisations a competitive advantage over those that don't.[11] The researchers found there was a strong correlation between a positive employee culture and good company performance, a high-quality product or service and excellent customer service. This was the case across a wide variety of industries.

Employee engagement doesn't just happen. Creating a positive emotional workplace culture requires constant attention to all the micro moments that characterise daily life in the office. Small but regular acts of kindness and support, for example, add up to an emotional culture characterised by compassion, caring, tenderness for others, joy, delight, a sense of pride and appreciation. In an environment like this, employees are more likely to demonstrate discretionary behaviours inside their organisation, actively advocating and supporting their colleagues.

However, if leaders err towards regular (albeit subtle) expressions of disappointment, anger or impatience, energy-draining emotions such as frustration, boredom, envy, fear and guilt will become deeply woven into the fabric of day-to-day interactions. Collaboration and decision making will rapidly descend into power plays, bullying and disillusionment. When energy-draining emotions dominate in the office, performance and retention will suffer greatly.

The goal here is, of course, to build and maintain a healthy emotional culture, which is one that produces strong and long-lasting positive emotions. All organisation leaders should constantly monitor and review features of the work environment which are related to healthy and to toxic emotional culture cultures. At HumanForce, we call this 'taking the pulse'.

Measures to test include the quality of the relationship between leaders, co-workers and employees, as well as wellbeing, diversity, openness and fairness. The process to do this might take the form of regular surveys or assessments of employees' perceptions of the workplace to discover whether they find it positive, respectful, inclusive, psychologically safe and trustworthy.

Is everybody *happy*?

Before we get into the detail of how to build a healthy emotional culture, let me first add a strong note of caution. You are most likely familiar with the device that uses a row of five button faces to express satisfaction. They are found everywhere from airports to restaurants. The buttons range from a sunshine yellow face with a broad smile (yeah, it was great!) to a dark red one with a deep frown (that was very below par). Press one on exit to register your feedback.

These buttons are increasingly being deployed in workplace lobbies, inviting employees to express their views on their workday as they leave each evening. They may sound like a bit of an HR gimmick, but they are seen to be a valuable tool in getting to know more about how employees are or want to be feeling. There is, however, a significant caveat here:

Organisations that decide to take up this idea should not be aiming for a 100% happiness score.

Granted, the goal of maintaining a wholly upbeat organisation is often undertaken with the best of intentions. Executives believe creating a smooth-running, pleasant environment to work in is helpful and encouraging for the team, but the outcome of this strategy is not always as they intended.

As I've already documented elsewhere in this book, we need a *balance* of emotions. It is not helpful to encourage (or worse still mandate) constant joy and happiness no matter what the situation. Energy-sapping emotions have something important to tell us about our leadership, team and company.

When a company's culture actively suppresses emotions it deems 'negative', it creates an environment of toxic positivity. This can be extremely harmful to the whole team because it makes individuals feel invalidated, unseen or unheard.

You may well recognise the signs of toxic positivity. This is where real emotions are actively suppressed through 'upbeat' phrases such as:

- 'Be positive!'

- 'Cheer up!'

- 'Look on the bright side!'

- 'It's all going to be OK!'

- 'Everything happens for a reason!'

- 'Stop being negative!'

- 'Think happy thoughts!'

In organisations where positivity is seen to be more valued than logic and there is a general feeling of forced happiness, multiple problems will escalate:

- Individuality will be suppressed since everyone is encouraged to fit into a rigid template of a typical happy employee, regardless of their own personality style.

- Employees will self-regulate their behaviour, meaning they brush crucial issues aside and withhold legitimate criticisms for fear of being seen as negative or an outlier.

- A lack of realism ensues. Individuals on the team will overestimate their own abilities, leading to over-optimism and a lack of preparation for events, meetings and presentations.

- Since criticism is frowned upon, this situation becomes self-perpetuating. Even terrible presentations will be applauded. This leads to a downwards spiral of poor performance.

- Meanwhile, under intense pressure to be happy, no one will feel that they can show their real selves at work. Emotions such as guilt, distrust and fear will be actively suppressed, leading to poor physical and mental health.

- Company-wide, morale and motivation will suffer since there are no obvious opportunities to improve.

- At the most extreme level, whistle-blowers and those who would stand up to injustice and prejudice are actively discouraged.

To avoid toxic positivity, create the space for *all* emotions. No one should feel they need to suppress any 'wrong' feelings.

Managers have a key role here in helping to validate their employees' experiences rather than encouraging them to bury them. Everyone should be trained to understand energy-sapping emotions and to air them where applicable so problems can be addressed head on, rather than hidden and allowed to fester. When there is an honest emotional culture, there is a far greater chance of identifying, tackling and solving issues, as well as having productive meetings with useful actionable feedback.

In the next three chapters, we will look in detail at how to build a balanced, healthy emotional culture based on confidence, trust and justice, with the goal of offering a place of psychological safety. This is the environment that will produce more energy-giving emotions such as joy, gratitude and hope, addressing feelings of connection, care and belonging. It's the key to true employee engagement.

Summary

When the word culture is used, most people think about *cognitive* culture. Cognitive culture describes the shared intellectual values, norms and assumptions that many organisations document in a bid to help their teams work together more effectively.

While cognitive culture is important, it only tells half the story. The other side to that story is *emotional* culture. Emotional culture is more focused on feelings, moods and attitudes.

Every organisation in every sector around the world has an emotional culture because they are staffed by human beings, and we are emotional. Business leaders who really want to get the best out of their employees need to go further than simply satisfying their basic human needs with smart offices and good working conditions. They need to build an emotional culture that recognises their *human* qualities as well.

TEN

A Culture Of Belonging

Everyone can remember a moment when they've felt like they haven't belonged. Maybe as a child at school, they felt like the outsider who never truly fitted in with the crowd. They may have always been among the last to be picked for a sports team or bullied for looking or acting 'different'. Perhaps they've moved to a new country or job and never quite managed to settle or they've felt the need to play down or hide their religious beliefs, accent or sexual orientation from those around them.

There are so many moments where we feel we don't fit in. I can vividly remember significant periods where I felt I didn't belong. Each time was for a slightly different reason, but they all impacted me with a deep sense of feeling set apart and wholly unsettled.

The first of these instances occurred during my childhood. I was born into a Jewish family, but my parents enrolled me into the local Church of England primary school, followed by a Church of England grammar school. Alongside my schooling, I went to Hebrew lessons and was encouraged to attend Jewish youth groups during my teen years.

During morning assemblies at school, I sang all the hymns. In lessons I focused my attention on religious education, learning more about the Christian religion than almost all my contemporaries, but I never felt quite at ease during the school assemblies and I never felt that I fitted in to the Jewish youth groups either. I felt sad that my school friends spent their time at the Christian youth groups without me. All of this left me with a sense of isolation.

When I started my legal career, it wasn't religion that set me apart, but background. I was employed by a prestigious law firm and it quickly became evident that the majority of my new colleagues came from a private-school background. I was transfixed by their relaxed air of privilege and entitlement, which was evident in all their daily interactions. It is something you simply don't learn at state schools.

Status, but of another sort, played a part in a period where yet again, I felt the outsider. This time, I had joined an organisation on a temporary contract. For some reason, I was kept on these terms for three whole years. This arrangement really took a toll because I never felt part of this organisation and the fact that all my colleagues were on permanent contracts only added to that impression of segregation. The feeling that I could never properly belong there played an instrumental part in my eventual resignation.

The need to belong

Why do we feel such a strong need to belong? Researcher Roy Baumeister says belonging, which he conceptualises broadly as a fundamental human need, is a complex construct due to its multifaceted components, predictors and outcomes.[1] His work goes beyond the simplistic notion that belonging is good and the absence of belonging is bad, suggesting that belonging is not only good, but the desire to belong is a deeply rooted human motivation. This motivation is underpinned by our ancestral origins, which permeate our thoughts, feelings and behaviours.

Another useful resource comes from researcher, speaker and author Brené Brown,[2] who has written extensively about the power of vulnerability. She says:

'We are biologically, cognitively, physically and spiritually wired to love, to be loved, and to belong. When those needs aren't met, we don't function as we were meant to be.'[3]

Brown is entirely right on the sheer breadth of the impact a feeling of belonging or *not* belonging can have upon us. We are hard-wired to feel anxious and uncomfortable if we believe we don't fit in. Our brains are constantly scanning and checking to see if we're being accepted by those around us.

When we do feel we have gained some approval, we get a reward response in our prefrontal cortex. Our brain processes feelings of acceptance in the same way as it does with feelings of love with a romantic partner. It produces potent hormones like dopamine, which are involved in reward, reinforcement and motivation. They make us feel good and encourage us to be engaged.

If, however, the conclusions of this scanning are that we don't fit in or have been rejected, a sense of threat and danger travels to the unconscious part of our brain. This activates our fight, flight or freeze response and can have a negative impact on our immune system and general health. The feeling of not belonging can be genuinely painful.

STUDY: Does rejection hurt?[4]

Social isolation is often described as 'hurt feelings', but does it really cause us the equivalent to physical pain? A group of researchers set up a neuroimaging study to find out if this was the case. Volunteers were scanned while playing Cyberball, a virtual ball-tossing game. While there was no direct social interaction between them, the participants believed they were playing the game with two others. In each case, the others stopped returning the ball, excluding the main player from the game.

The scan results showed that when the volunteers were excluded, their anterior cingulate cortex and right ventral prefrontal cortex were more active, correlating to their reports of distress and pain at being ignored and left out.

We have talked a lot about EQ, but there is another element at play which impacts our sense of belonging: cultural intelligence. As psychologist Paul Ekman observed, people from different cultures differ in the way they display and express emotion.[5] This has an impact on today's more diverse humanforces because while we all *feel* the same emotions such as anger, fear, joy and sadness, the way different cultures *interpret*, control and express their emotions will differ.

In each culture, there are unwritten rules and norms about which emotions are acceptable in certain situations and which are not. In Western cultures, people tend to more readily and vocally express the high-energy emotions such as anger and passion. It is culturally acceptable to show enthusiasm in a meeting. However, those from some Asian cultures prefer to voice their emotions in a more muted, reserved way. Similarly, in Western cultures, individualism is encouraged, whereas other cultures favour working collectively.

If business leaders do not understand these norms and that the behaviour of a person in a group may be different from the others, it is easy for them to exclude that person. Just because one individual in the group does not appear enthusiastic doesn't mean they are not keen – they simply may not be disposed to showing intense emotions. Meanwhile, that same individual may feel they have to adjust their behaviour to maintain harmony in their group, adding to their feeling of being the outsider.

STUDY: Universals and cultural differences in the judgements of facial expressions of emotion[6]

Are facial expressions universal? Apparently, only when we are being watched.

In this study, Japanese and American subjects were asked to watch stress-inducing films. When the subjects watched the films alone, they had broadly the same facial responses, but when they were told they were being observed, the Japanese masked their negative expressions with smiles, concealing their true feelings.

Why belonging and connection are so important in the workplace

We live in uncertain times. In the search for some comfort and stability, many individuals have great expectations from their workplaces. They are looking for an oasis, a place of safety where they can find a sense of meaning and solidarity.

It's a trend that has not gone unrecognised. According to one survey, 79% of organisations say fostering a sense of belonging is important to their future success.[7] When employees feel they are being respected and treated fairly, it has a positive impact on all areas of the working day. A sense of belonging can lead to a 56% improvement in job performance, a 50% reduction in turnover risk and a 75% decrease in employee sick days. Even just one incident that leaves a member of the team feeling excluded or out on a limb can lead to an immediate 25% drop in that individual's performance.

The obvious question is: how well are employers' efforts to encourage belonging going? Not very well, if reports from the frontline are anything to go by. The majority of employees don't feel they belong in their workplace. One survey showed that 61% of workers feel obliged to conceal their true selves at work, engaging in 'covering', a term coined by sociologist Erving Goffman.[8] The mask people create for themselves when they feel they don't belong can be anything from altering their personality to the clothes they wear to the way they speak. In each case, the goal is the same: to assimilate and therefore fit in.

Covering takes its toll. When we feel compelled to act out of character for long periods or to be someone else, it reduces job satisfaction, increases stress and can even lead to burnout. When those in leadership roles behave in this way, the problem can be compounded. Under pressure to perform, they may become inconsistent and erratic, trialling different behaviours to fit in with how they perceive they should be, but never feeling they quite get it right. Meanwhile, their direct reports will become confused and unsettled by the constant mixed messages.

When people are masking, it is not always immediately obvious. You may be familiar with the term 'emotional labour'. It was a bit of a buzzword in 2018, initially used to describe the need to suppress our emotions at work, particularly in challenging customer-facing roles where team members are expected to remain calm and pleasant, whatever the situation.

More recently, it has been expanded to describe the process of pretending we are not at all bothered by microaggression in the workplace. We're talking here about those subtle digs with undertones of sexism, racism, ableism and so much more. Often dressed up as 'banter', these repeated slights all add together to destroy the sense of belonging for the person on the other end of them.

Our desire to belong is driven by a need for strong social connections. When we are connected, we feel we belong. In the workplace, this is where the magic can really happen when leaders are creating a positive emotional culture. Strong social connections lead to increased flows in communication and co-operation. As a result, people find their jobs satisfying and are resilient to the stresses and strains of the workplace, which in turn increases their commitment to their employers. Together, they can all work at a high level.

The opposite is also true. When we don't experience a social connection at work, it has a negative impact on our employee experience. Workers who feel lonely and isolated are less productive than their counterparts, their work can be of a lower quality and they are likely to take additional days' leave due to chronic stress and illness.

According to the *British Medical Journal*, loneliness carries with it a series of negative health impacts including increased risk of coronary heart disease and stroke, issues with the immune system and cognitive decline.[9] The impact is not dissimilar to a smoker with a fifteen-cigarette-a-day habit. Conversely, when we have strong emotional connections, they are believed to lead to a long lifespan and resilience over disease and stress.

A culture of connection and belonging is closely linked to the notion of psychological safety: the belief that we are not an embarrassment or at risk of rejection. When people feel they are psychologically safe, that they belong and are respected by their peers, they will be more confident about sharing their ideas, even if those ideas seem a little crazy at first glance. Those crazy ideas may just turn into winners. Wouldn't it be a huge loss if people didn't feel safe enough to speak up?

The growth in the sense of disconnection from our workplace has accelerated in recent times. First there was the pandemic, which saw many people working remotely for long periods. Now we have entered a new era of hybrid working with countless numbers combining working from home and the office. As a result, many people are feeling isolated and the challenge around creating a sense of belonging has been amplified. How do we as leaders achieve this for those who rarely or only occasionally come into face-to-face contact with their co-workers?

The paradox we all face is, despite the many different forms of social media, along with a plethora of ways to communicate remotely, from text to email to (old-fashioned!) phone calls, many of us feel lonelier than ever. We are connected in a technological way, yet not in a personal sense. In recent times, this has been one of the most significant problems I come across when I work with teams, particularly those that work at home or in a hybrid way.

A report by CIGNA in early 2022 showed 61% of employees feel lonely, up 7% points in five years.[10] People who report feeling disconnected from their colleagues and from their managers are 10% lonelier than those who do not (53% versus 43%). In Chapter One, we explored the Great Resignation. I suspect that we will soon be hearing a lot about the Great Disconnection as the loneliness epidemic really takes hold.

A significant part of the problem is there is still a stigma around loneliness. Most people are unwilling to admit that they feel set apart from their colleagues or that they're not a proper functioning part of the team. Once they grow used to wearing a mask at work, they become increasingly less likely to speak up. Often, by the time managers realise team members feel this way, their key people will have resigned and it will be too late to do anything about it.

Diversity, inclusion and belonging

The case for diversity and inclusion in the workplace is stronger than ever. It is now widely understood and accepted that diverse organisations outperform their counterparts on every metric, from financial to engagement to creativity and innovation.[11] When people feel their differences and uniqueness are valued, it boosts an organisation's hiring and retention potential.

In recent times, the words diversity and inclusion, which have for so long been linked together, have been joined by another one: belonging. Numerous articles on LinkedIn or books on leadership point to the combined power of these three ideals, but while the intention is good, lumping them all into one catch-all term can be counterproductive. Just because someone is *included* in an organisation, it doesn't follow that they feel like they belong.

Diversity, inclusion and belonging (DIB) are *incremental* steps in shaping a successful modern workplace. Diversity is about representation in the humanforce spanning race, ethnicity, gender, age, religion and physical ability. Either an organisation has a diverse humanforce or it doesn't.

Once an organisation has established a diverse humanforce, its leaders need to make an effort to ensure everyone feels included. Inclusion is a behaviour, where a mix of people can come into the workplace and feel comfortable and confident to be themselves, knowing that their perspective is valued.

The feeling of belonging takes this ideal one step further. Belonging is the emotional outcome an organisation gets when its people feel they are part of a community and that their differences are treasured.

I like the way that Pat Waders, Chief People Officer at UKG, puts it. She says that, 'D&I may capture your head, but belonging captures your heart'.[12] If we put it another way, diversity is a fact (the numbers), inclusion is a choice (we decide whether to include someone or not), but belonging is a feeling that is enforced by the culture we purposely create in our workplaces.

If we don't get each stage of this right, it can damage all our efforts and best intentions. Firms can make great inroads into recruiting under-represented groups to create a more diverse humanforce, but if these employees are then made to feel like they don't fit in, it will be to everyone's disadvantage.

Earlier, I mentioned emotional labour. This can be even more pronounced for people of colour or who are LGBTQ+ or have a disability, or indeed any under-represented group that will encounter uncomfortable or even offensive situations surprisingly often. Not only will they need to deal with it on a personal level, but there also tends to be an organisation-wide expectation they will respond politely and be willing to correct and teach colleagues. Day by day, this undermines everything that an organisation is doing to create a more diverse humanforce.

Certain team members will inevitably feel like they need to come to work wearing a protective mask, pretending to be who they are not, to fit in. Reports show 83% of LGBTQ+, 79% of black and 66% of women employees make efforts to cover their identities.[13] As we've discussed, this can impact these employees' health and wellbeing, the way they feel about work and how they contribute. Meanwhile, the benefits of diversity will not be realised for employers, because when no one is able to bring their real self into the workplace, it is impossible to realise the full potential of their talent.

Organisations' DIB strategies need to make sure people feel they belong and can be their authentic selves. Don't forget that in today's global humanforce, we are not just considering how teams work together in a single office. Many teams span the world, so there may well be multiple different cultures, backgrounds and attitudes to consider when it comes to thinking about how to foster a sense of belonging in each member of the team so they feel empowered to fully contribute.

Emotional work and EQ can be the glue. They're also necessary elements to make DIB efforts successful. Companies are undertaking a lot of work to put in place practices, policies and measurements, including recruitment targets around diversity and inclusion. All of this is necessary, but let's not forget that DIB is about human beings and ultimately it is a personal, emotional subject. Building EQ among employees and leaders will be the factor that helps people to change behaviour and individuals to feel that they belong. Every person must respect others' individuality and connect and communicate to build that inclusive culture.

Much of what I have described in this book is relevant to DIB efforts. The self-awareness that we focused on in Chapter Three helps employees observe and identify their emotions in certain situations, as well as assess how they feel about a topic that may involve bias or make them feel uncomfortable, so they don't shy away from that discomfort. Being able to identify the emotions that are brought up in us by others is key to self-management. Our success in working in this way will have a huge impact on inclusivity.

Empathy will also be key to increasing a sense of belonging. Active listening and being able to interact with those who have different backgrounds or viewpoints will help to break down silos and unite teams.

Some organisations are already making great inroads here, building on the emotional side by encouraging storytelling. This is where there are exchanges of human experience via employee representative groups, focus groups and listening sessions that inspire and move people to act. Stories open up conversations, invite perspective, taking and help people to stand in someone else's shoes. Indeed, one study found that taking the perspective of others may have a 'lasting positive effect on diversity-related outcomes by increasing individuals' internal motivation to respond without prejudice'.[14]

Rubén Alejandro, Group Head Diversity and Inclusion, Syngenta Group

When I posted my own coming-out story to the Syngenta population, it got about 22,000 views. People got in touch to say how they'd been positively impacted by my openness. The majority of the people in the company are straight, but many have children or friends in my position and can relate to it. My situation was personal to me, but by presenting it in the way I did, I helped others to speak more openly and to listen properly too.

Of course, the success of these storytelling initiatives depends upon the creation of a safe space for employees to talk and express themselves without fear of retribution. Some companies might need to hire external facilitators to moderate listening sessions and deal with sensitive topics.

Building meaningful connections

Connecting our teams is not something that will just fall into place because we have embraced a new way of hybrid or remote working. It won't even happen for those who return to the office full time for business as usual. Working as a group, whether face to face or via regular Teams or Zoom meetings, doesn't mean we are creating meaningful associations. It doesn't automatically confer a feeling of being understood, appreciated and accepted, nor does it follow that people will be emboldened to offer diverse perspectives.

We need to give careful thought to how we embrace technology in the workplace, because it can have a significant impact on our teams' feeling of connection and belonging. When our predominant means of communication is via technology, it is easy for people to feel at a distance emotionally. Employees are then far less likely to talk about things that fall outside of work or to open up about themselves or ask for support, because there is a sense that employers don't care about them as human beings. When these essential parts of communication are pushed to one side, loneliness will always ensue.

Likewise, in this tech-heavy 24/7 culture with its constant barrage of information, it is easy for people to feel overwhelmed and overloaded. Dealing with work tasks will routinely take precedence over fostering human connections. You may not realise it is happening, but it is. If, say, you've found yourself checking and responding to emails at the weekend instead of enjoying time with family and friends, then you are missing out on an important emotional side to your life and day-to-day realities.

It's been referred to as an 'information tennis match'. We are engrossed in the perpetual volleying of ideas and opinions, but not taking the time to get to know one another.

Moving an organisation towards a culture of belonging will take time. Not everything will work first time; some actions might feel clumsy and contrived. Mistakes may be made, but if leaders are transparent in what they are trying to do and sincere in their intent, things will change. The dial will shift from employees feeling included towards feeling they belong.

In this last section, let's look at some ideas for how to actively build a culture of belonging into our organisations.

Use technology wisely

Technology has been a fantastic development for the corporate world, offering a huge range of benefits from speeding up production processes to making teams more efficient, but we need to think carefully about the extent to which we use it. It's easy to send an email or WhatsApp message to convey a point about a work issue, but this can get in the way of building and maintaining meaningful social relationships.

You as leader need to model the way by regularly picking up the phone or, even better, stopping by someone's desk to deliver a message in person. Face-to-face communication helps people feel less lonely and disconnected. It creates a sense of belonging and a close affiliation with the workplace. Where possible, hold discussions over an informal cup of coffee or lunch, or a brief stroll around the block.

Engineer some in-office social-connection days

Even if the majority of your work is done remotely, engineer days when the entire team can be in the office together. Make it a firm ritual placed in everyone's diary rather than a vague date in the future when 'we must get everyone together'. It can help to give the event a hook like 'Storytelling Friday' when each week an employee will be invited to tell a personal story. Origin stories are powerful ways of creating belonging.

An alternative might be 'Gratitude Mondays' where a few members of the team can kick off the week by describing something they are grateful for. Remember, the purpose of these events is *not* to talk only about work. They give people the chance to connect from a purely human standpoint.

Remote doesn't need to mean fully disconnected

When face-to-face contact is not possible, make a deliberate effort to ensure everyone can still have that personal connection. Use collaboration tools such as Flock, Google Chat and Slack to their full capacity.

This chat shouldn't be confined to the day job either. Encourage colleagues to set a time to have a coffee break together online, so they can talk with one another in the same way as they might during a break in the office. They could even go for a walk together while chatting on smartphones. It may feel a little awkward at first, but then again, so did video conferences when we first started to use them. They are like second nature for most of us now.

A useful ice breaker can be to organise a 'book of the month' event. The book can be on a subject close to the nature of your business or simply the latest page-turner. The goal is to encourage the whole team to read the book and comment on it, setting in place an opportunity to interact.

Another option might be peer-to-peer mentoring programmes where different teams can get to know one another and help one another out with particular activities. This cross-functional communication is very effective. Curiosity about others and what they do is a great way to build a deep bond. Along the way, teams will get to know more about the likes, dislikes and motivations of others and, if they want to share it, a bit more about them as a person.

Maintain open lines of communication

The idea of an open-door policy might seem a little dated now, especially when teams are often apart, but you can reiterate that the concept still stands, albeit on slightly different terms. Make it clear to teams that the lines of communication are very much open, whatever the medium. If anyone wants to jump online for a chat or to raise concerns, they will be welcome. There are no limitations on what can be discussed, either. Regular, honest feedback is the foundation for good communications and can really increase connection.

Returning to the issue of cultural awareness, consider having a conversation with members of the group about the emotions they're using in interactions. Ask them what they feel comfortable with. If they are not the type to jump up and down with enthusiasm at each new announcement, that's fine. You just need to be prepared for that and plan your interactions accordingly.

Welcome new team members

While many employees may have made friends among colleagues prior to the prevalence of remote and hybrid working arrangements, the same can't be said for new team members. Therefore, pay particular attention to onboarding processes. Virtual onboarding is fine if handled well, but it often isn't and this can be a problem. This is, after all, a crucial first opportunity for people to make friends and feel connected with their new workplace.

Put in place a process within your organisation where new team members can be introduced to all their colleagues and get to know them relatively quickly in as informal a setting as possible. An 'onboarding buddy' might be useful as they can help new recruits by offering support and insights where needed, and making them feel safe and welcome.

Create activities outside work

Creating a sense of belonging doesn't need to be confined to the office. As Anne Sophie says here, working together on a common mission or purpose can be just as powerful because it gives the team something to take pride in collectively.

> **Anne Sophie Eyméoud, Director General of Rothschild & Co Wealth Management, Belgium**
>
> Building sincere links and opportunities for the team to share mutual experiences creates a culture of caring and belonging. Encouraging everyone to work together for a day on philanthropic activities, such as helping young or disadvantaged groups, creates a deep connection among the team. Investing in the wider community is inspiring in so many ways.

Share news

Finally, introduce a mechanism to give everyone regular updates on how the company is getting on. What's new? How are specific projects faring? Who has achieved something worth noting? Employees will feel more connected to their companies if they feel included in currents events.

Support all of these activities with a system that regularly checks in with members of the team to take the pulse of how everyone feels. This check-in process might take the form of surveys or group chats with the aim of finding out whether people feel they belong. The actual mechanism is up to you and the processes your company favours. The important thing is to build it into the day-to-day routine.

Summary

Why is belonging so crucial to a human's wellbeing? We are hard-wired to feel anxious and uncomfortable if we believe we don't fit in. Our brains are constantly scanning and checking to see if we're being accepted by those around us. When we do feel we have gained some approval, our brain produces potent hormones like dopamine, which are involved in reward, reinforcement and motivation. They make us feel good and encourage us to be engaged.

If, however, the conclusions of this scanning are that we don't fit in or have been rejected, a sense of threat and danger travels to the unconscious part of our brain. This activates our fight, flight or freeze response and can have a negative impact on our immune system and general health. The feeling of not belonging can be genuinely painful.

ELEVEN

A Culture Of Care

Float the idea of love in the workplace and you may well receive a raised eyebrow in response. Someone might even mutter, 'There are rules against that type of thing!' While it is now more widely accepted than it was that emotions have a role to play in effective leadership, it's rare to find the word 'love' in a corporate context.

Just for a moment, forget the notion of romantic love and think instead of all the other emotions associated with a mutually beneficial close relationship. Consider the intense feelings of affection, compassion, caring, loyalty and tenderness for others that characterise love. Now imagine how powerful these emotions could prove if carefully nurtured in the workplace.

STUDY: What's love got to do with it?[1]

Beginning with the healthcare industry, the research team for this study set out to identify whether an environment of compassionate love had an impact on employee morale and effectiveness. It transpired that employees who felt deeply valued in this way were more engaged, less emotionally exhausted and more satisfied with their jobs than those who didn't. This was, in turn, appreciated by customers, specifically patients and their families, who reported an increase in pleasant moods, satisfaction with their treatment and the quality of life they experienced.

Compassionate love and caring might be felt to be a prerequisite in a healthcare setting, so the correlation between this and employee and customer satisfaction was examined in other unrelated industries. At first sight, the results were less than conclusive. There was a variation in levels of compassion depending upon the sector, but the most significant variations were within sectors themselves. Some organisations in, say, the financial services industry rated as highly as those in the healthcare industry, while others in this sector rated very low indeed. Despite its proven effectiveness, compassionate love is a question of choice within corporate culture.

When we have a close, caring friendship with another individual, whether at work or socially, we become much more relaxed about saying what we really think and feel than we do with anyone else we know on a more casual footing. We will voice opinions we might otherwise keep to ourselves because we trust this other person enough to know they won't immediately knock the thought down or belittle us.

Over time, this authenticity and openness between two people has the potential to develop into a deep, emotional connection. We will feel safe in conveying our vulnerabilities or admitting to making mistakes. The feeling will be reciprocated too. We are all inclined to show support and empathy for someone we are close to when they are in need.

Consider how powerful it would be if you felt emboldened to converse in a similar way with all your colleagues. It seems inevitable that this honest environment would improve everyone's performance and creativity. Think about how much more fruitful discussions will become when no one feels the need to dance around any issues for fear of saying the wrong thing.

John McCusker, Global Vice President of Talent Management, Bacardi

There are three magical things that every leader can do. One is to ask everyone on their team how they are. Two is to properly listen to the answer and three is to care about what has just been said. If every leader did that, we wouldn't be talking about the Great Resignation any more.

When people feel happy to talk, unhindered and unconcerned by the optics, they do not fear sharing their infallibilities. We all have infallibilities and we all make mistakes. It is extremely healthy to share them, particularly in the workplace. When failure is not immediately derided or punished, but rather openly explored, it can quickly be fixed rather than brushed under the carpet where it has the potential to grow into an even bigger problem. Not only that, everyone will get the opportunity to learn from the mistake too. When mistakes and failure are a normal part of everyday work, organisations become innovative and creative.

Not surprisingly, a growing number of businesses are picking up on the power of caring. A Google search of company values and principles reveals a wide range of organisations that put the words 'love' and 'care' at the forefront of their culture. Household names such as PepsiCo, Whole Foods and Southwest Airlines are among them.

Embracing the power of caring could be the culmination of the shift away from a company culture driven by the needs of the boardroom and wholly concerned with productivity and efficiency, and towards one where considering employees is of paramount importance. Rather than seeing the team as assets who are simply there to get the job done, a broad range of organisation leaders accept the value of showing that they genuinely care about them as individuals.

When employees feel cared for, 60% are likely to stick with an organisation for three or more years.[2] This is as opposed to just 7% who don't feel cared for, but still said they would likely stay for the same period. As for feeling included, 95% of those who felt cared for said they counted, against 14% whose feelings were neglected. A similar gulf in responses could be found among those who would recommend their employers to others (90% who felt cared for versus 9% who didn't) and those who were personally engaged with work (94% versus 43%). Even those who admitted to feeling under stress believed they were better able to manage it with the support of their employers (50% compared to 14%).

Why we need care in the workplace

One of the many outcomes of the pandemic was that vast numbers of us had time to think about our lives and the direction we've chosen. Lengthy periods of isolation encouraged us to recognise our own self-worth, spanning all areas from our personal values and purpose at home to our choice of work. Plenty of people questioned whether they wanted to be a wage slave in a job that they didn't care much about with an employer who didn't care much about them.

We talked earlier about the Great Resignation; well, you could say the Great Reflection has become one of the key triggers for the mass movement to switch jobs and search for something better. The obvious conclusion is: employers who don't care or don't show they care are going to be on the back foot in the war for talent.

At the height of the pandemic, most employers got this. Certainly, the services of my company were more in demand than they ever had been. With a large number of teams working from home, numerous organisations recognised that while digital communication was a lifesaver when it came to keeping in touch and carrying on business largely as usual, it did mean caring and compassion had become a bit of a casualty.

When the opportunity to bump into colleagues on a day-to-day basis is removed, it takes conscious effort to remember to stop and chat or catch up, or to pause to practise some old-fashioned gratitude. When we're working remotely, we often don't see people from one day to the next, other than as a two-dimensional image on screen. Meetings get run to schedule and there is little chance for small talk, particularly if a number of people are involved in each interaction. One-to-one asides simply don't work well in this medium.

Most employers were also quick to recognise the dangers of this during the health crisis as we all adapted to a new way of working. There was a widespread recognition that if organisations did not act and properly look after the emotional needs of their teams, they could well face a second epidemic: burnout. Now the pandemic is behind us and everyone is 'back to normal', there are signs that some employers are quietly dropping all the self-awareness stuff. If this is the case in your organisation, you are sorely misjudging the situation. Many people are still working at home or via a hybrid model and facing the same challenges of loneliness and isolation.

Meanwhile, the countless numbers who discovered their purpose during lockdowns, or at least were on the way to doing so, are unlikely to accept returning to the pre-pandemic status quo. Perhaps most importantly, stress and burnout have not gone away. They are still on the rise.

As I have been writing this book, numerous reports have surfaced around the levels of wellbeing and mental health in the world. The Mental Health at Work

Report 2022, which carried out interviews with over 3,000 employees, found that three in four people are currently experiencing mental-health issues at work and a startling one in seven are leaving their workplace due to mental-health issues related to work.[3] These are sobering facts.

Earlier, we looked at the toll of the pandemic on mental health and wellbeing, and the rise of chronic stress and burnout worldwide. Having worked with many organisations to build healthy cultures, supporting their employees during stressful transitions, I am still astounded by the lack of understanding about what causes burnout and how to tackle it properly.

Companies are failing to address the root causes of burnout, which is a systemic problem often linked to a toxic working environment, inflexible workloads, a squeeze on staffing and resources, and unreasonable expectations. It's not enough for company leaders to say they are committed to health and wellbeing and to give coaching and gym membership. Burnout is a significant problem that needs to be properly addressed and it is the responsibility of every organisation to do this, taking real, active steps towards its prevention.

One of the problems with chronic stress is it's not always immediately obvious. Individuals suffering from stress may appear to be functioning well, coming to work normally and carrying out their usual duties, but inside they can be falling apart. There are many reasons to create a caring culture, but this is one of the strongest.

When a company has a caring culture, symptoms of chronic stress will be picked up on quickly and easily.

Team leaders will have awareness of the mental health and wellbeing in their workplace, meaning they can react quickly as soon as they notice such symptoms.

Creating a caring culture

At the broadest level, caring can be defined as providing others with health, welfare and protection, but in a corporate setting, caring needs to be wider than this. If you were to consider the concept of caring in the context of the Maslow Hierarchy of Needs,[4] which we touched on in Chapter Two, it would sit firmly on the second tier: safety. Our need to be cared for in all areas of our lives, including work, runs parallel with our desire to feel safe.

Maslow's Hierarchy of Needs

In Chapter Five, when we talked about leading with emotion, we explored how crucial it is that leaders create a safe emotional space. I suggested using techniques such as active listening to properly pay attention to what people are saying, as well as creating safe spaces so everyone feels emboldened to talk freely. This all helps ensure that employees feel safe to express their feelings to one another and their team leaders without fear of any judgement or repercussion. When leaders create an environment like this, it goes a long way towards making employees feel cared for and open to sharing thoughts and concerns they might otherwise have kept to themselves.

There is more that we can do. While it is crucial to create an emotional safe space in the workplace, it is equally crucial to remember people's lives do not just centre around work. Caring is about creating a relationship and, as we all know, one-sided relationships or those where we don't really make the effort to get to know one another never work out well.

Leaders need to show they care about each of their team members' whole self. In other words, the focus is on employees' life experience, the person they are at home and at play, as well as in work. None of us become different people the moment we walk into the workplace and sit down at our desks, and nor should we. We are whole human beings and need to be seen as such. This is the basis for bringing our whole selves to work.

What, then, is the problem? Perhaps it is a relic of the time when kindness and compassion were seen as a weakness in the workplace. As the proverb goes: 'Nice people finish last.' Being caring is the antithesis of the super-competitive crush-the-opposition entrepreneurial behaviour that has long been lauded. Fortunately, we have started to see a shift in the right direction, where organisation leaders are at least talking about fostering a culture of kindness, albeit with a way to go.

Again, this recognition of an employee as a whole person is something the majority want to see happen. According to research, 82% of employees say it is important for them that their organisation sees them as a complete person, but also again, many employers are falling short on this ideal.[5] Less than half (45%) of employees feel their organisation treats them in this way.

There is more. There's a lack of understanding about what being seen as a complete person means. Most of us are concerned about multiple things that exist beyond the four walls of our workplaces and many of these things concern those closest to us. In the same research, more than 60% of employees said it's important for their employers to recognise and understand their personal commitments, families and communities and, even better, to be willing to make accommodations where possible. However, at the moment, the majority of employers are falling short. Just 37% said that their organisation had any understanding of what employees need in their personal life and for their families.

Creating a caring culture requires a top-down approach. This is not something that a little resource can be thrown at, letting others further down the hierarchy deal with the 'touchy feely' stuff (although it must be said, too many organisations don't even set aside enough of a budget to deal with it). It is not simply an HR problem. Leaders need to model the way if they want to create a caring culture. After all, they are, or at least should be, the first in line when it comes to noticing signs of stress or anxiety in individual team members.

Leaders may well need to begin this process with training in how to prioritise mental health and well-being. This will help them to navigate the sometimes delicate conversations that go with the process of helping others to open up and speak freely. Often, this training will require leaders themselves to become comfortable about sharing personal information with their teams to encourage others to speak openly.

In the early days, people may find it difficult to get used to a caring culture at work. Like any new relationship, it takes time to build trust and a close bond. Sometimes, this relationship might need a bit of coaxing to move it forward.

In a corporate setting, this is especially so when it comes to creating an environment where it is cool to talk about mistakes. If the previous norm was to come down heavily on anyone making a mistake, employees will be naturally suspicious.

Is this a trap? Am I going to admit all, then get into trouble?

As in the previous chapter on belonging and connection, the initial solutions might at first glance seem a little contrived, but people will get used to them. Over time, they will become part of the routine.

One such solution is Failure Fridays, which have been adopted by a number of organisations such as the digital firm PagerDuty. This is where time is set aside each week to talk about certain projects and analyse how they went, with a particular emphasis on what could have been done better. These failures don't need to be catastrophic (hopefully there won't be enough of those sorts of failures to discuss). They are simply the hiccups along the way that slowed things down or set things off on an unnecessary side tangent.

The idea is not to name and shame, but to get the whole team to put forward ideas on ways to avoid making the same mistake twice. There should also be no bar on talking about successes at these sessions. Storytelling or story sharing, whether around successes or failures, is the key to creating transparency in an organisation. This honesty is the foundation of a trusting, caring relationship.

When you're creating a caring environment, don't miss any opportunity. During one-on-one meetings to discuss progress on a particular project, either online or face to face, begin or end the discussion with some personal chat. These getting-to-know-you conversations can span everything from what the employee got up to at the weekend to how their family members are doing to progress on their training regime towards the triathlon they once mentioned.

Little acts of kindness go a long way. We talked earlier about saying thank you and showing appreciation, but this can be extended to dropping by a colleague's desk with a cup of coffee now and again. Taking along two cups is a good excuse to stop for a moment or two while you both sip your coffee and catch up.

STUDY: The reinforcing benefits of giving, getting and glimpsing[6]

The concept of pay it forward says that when someone does something for you, instead of paying that person back directly, you pass it on to another person instead. Can simple acts of kindness in the workplace create a more caring culture? Research by the team from the University of California seems to indicate that this is so.

A group of workers from Coca Cola in Madrid were divided up into givers and receivers. The givers were asked to conduct five acts of kindness towards the receivers over a period of four weeks. These acts could be anything from bringing a co-worker a drink to giving some words of encouragement to someone who appeared to be having a bad day. The receivers were unaware that the givers had been given the assignment.

Both givers and receivers were noticeably happier at the end of the experiment. In addition, the givers' positive acts encouraged the receivers to do the same. In other words, the receivers paid the givers' acts of kindness forward. Caring and kindness are contagious.

One of my clients, who places 'caring' at the top of her agenda, keeps notes in her diary of her team members' birthdays, anniversaries and any other important dates. If someone is unwell in her team, she puts reminders in her diary to check in with them regularly to see how they feel.

Creating a caring, listening culture may require a multi-stage approach, beginning with building deeper connections than you have now by talking more openly with employees at appropriate opportunities. You can then build upon these efforts by offering employees more flexibility in their work timetables to accommodate any unexpected crises arising at home. There could, for example, be an initiative to offer extended family leave in certain circumstances. Alternatively, you could introduce parent support groups as a valuable network for new mums and dads.

If, through the new regime of deep, personal conversations, you learn that an individual has a particular hobby or skill that they are interested in developing, you could look for opportunities to step in and support this aspiration for personal growth. It could be that fostering this interest and helping the individual to develop their skill will be mutually compatible with what's being pursued in the workplace. Even if this is not necessarily the case, it will be extremely motivating to the person involved to see they are getting the support they crave to lead a well-rounded and fulfilling life. Pay attention to holistic wellbeing, looking after hearts and minds to create an atmosphere of shared purpose.

Finally, you could look closely at the working week. A number of European companies in countries including the UK, Iceland and Belgium are conducting trials of a four-day working week. The initiative crosses organisations in a range of sectors, from online book and gift shop Bookishly to AKA Case Management. The idea is that employees work four days a week, completing the same workload while getting paid the same and earning the same benefits as they would in the traditional five-day week.

In another experiment along the same lines, companies in Sweden trialled a six-hour workday instead of the usual eight hours.[7] While it is early on in this initiative and there have been some detractors, the feedback from employees has been largely positive. Chronic stress and burnout have reduced and workers report a much improved work-life balance.

When we are kind to people and we care for them, thinking about every aspect of their life, including their health and wellbeing, it can transform the environment for both employers and employees.

Summary

Introduce the idea of love in the workplace and you may well receive a raised eyebrow in response. While it is now more widely accepted that emotions have a role to play in effective leadership, it's rare to find the word 'love' in a corporate context.

Just for a moment, forget the notion of romantic love and think instead of all the other emotions associated with a mutually beneficial close relationship. Consider the intense feelings of affection, compassion, caring, loyalty and tenderness for others that characterise love. Now imagine how powerful these emotions could prove if carefully nurtured in the workplace.

TWELVE
A Culture Of Recognition And Appreciation

If I were to identify a theme that I hear most often in my coaching sessions, it would be that people don't feel valued. Despite all their best efforts, they believe their work isn't appreciated or often even noticed. The irony is when I speak with managers, they are usually quite convinced they are on top of this, dishing out praise left, right and centre. After all, it's the norm these days for most companies to give extensive training on how to deliver positive feedback.

I hesitate to take one side or the other, but I will share my experience here and leave you to make up your own mind about how good company leaders are at showing their appreciation. I can remember in great detail the handful of times that I received praise from a boss or colleague during my working life. I could almost tell you the exact words that were used.

This tells me two things: it didn't happen very often and when it did, it made a *huge* impression upon me.

We talked earlier about the power of a simple thank you. It's something that takes literally seconds to say and doesn't cost anything, yet it doesn't happen nearly enough. When leaders say thank you often, a good feeling will permeate their organisation, creating trust and a lasting connection.

We all crave recognition. When our efforts are celebrated, it stimulates activity in one part of the brain, the hypothalamus, which controls eating, sleeping and stress levels, activating the pleasure hormone dopamine. This makes us feel good and motivates us to do more of whatever it was that got us that positive response.

In a business setting, it's to everyone's advantage to create a culture of recognition and appreciation. When people feel their efforts have been noticed, it encourages positivity, which in turn enhances the overall positive culture in the workplace. This has an impact on engagement and performance too.

The opposite is also true. Surveys put 'feeling disrespected at work' in the top three reasons for why employees quit jobs.[1] Feeling disrespected (57%) is just behind low pay (63%) and no opportunities for advancement (63%).

My suspicion is that the gulf between how companies believe they are giving out praise and the reality has its roots in the difference between recognition and appreciation. Recognition is the praise that is given in response to an accomplishment, such as getting good results or seeing a project through to a successful conclusion. Appreciation, on the other hand, is more connected with an individual's value and worth as a human being. We appreciate someone for who they are and for what they contribute, rather than the end product or results that they achieve.

Both recognition and appreciation are crucial to employee engagement. For example, when an employee feels unappreciated, it creates a strong enough response to make them consider quitting a job. Research shows that nearly half of American workers (46%) have left a job because they feel unappreciated, while 65% said they'd work harder if only their contribution was recognised by their bosses.[2]

While business leaders should focus on *both* recognition and appreciation, most err towards showing recognition, celebrating the big wins. If you were to play this out to its logical conclusion, you might say that the reason there is such a drought in praise is that there is always a bit of a gap between one big achievement and the next. Those significant moments where a tender is won or a project completed may be stretched out over weeks and months before there is a tangible result to make a big deal about. Notwithstanding there will be many small wins during that period, which also deserve recognition, this means that most team members will spend months and months without a word of praise.

Meanwhile, by not even considering appreciation, many leaders are missing out on countless opportunities to connect with their team as individuals.

Previously, we talked about the dangers of a loss of connection. When we show our appreciation as leaders, we build that connection and a sense of belonging too. It strengthens our relationship with our teams.

Recognising the small wins all the way through a project is powerful, not least because some people don't necessarily want to be recognised because they have had a result. It is far better to focus on the *process* that leads to that result. Think of a team that has achieved a 10% increase in sales. The result is, of course, impressive, but it came about because of the way the team leader motivated their team members, the way in which they all worked together and the extra hours they put in. The result is the collective impact of all these inputs, but leaders need to recognise the effort put into achieving it.

Even just a few words of recognition along the way can be super impactful and remembered for years to come. One of my fondest memories of my childhood is when my piano teacher told me that she was very proud of the effort that I always put into my practice. When she showed appreciation by adding that I was one of her favourite students, I was on cloud nine for weeks afterwards. I can still remember the rush of adrenalin and pride when she said this. Bear in mind that each time I passed the next grade in line, I was always rewarded with a certificate to put on my wall. While they were nice certificates, their value paled in comparison to how good I felt after my piano teacher said those words.

If your boss has ever said anything to you like 'You are such a lovely person to work with' or 'You bring such a nice vibe to the team', you will know how amazing this feels and you won't forget it. It's just so personal to you as an individual.

Needless to say, showing appreciation is not a task that can be farmed out to someone else to take care of. It is not the responsibility of HR, akin to some sort of monetary benefit or reward. Leaders need to take an active role in the process.

I love the story of Campbell Soup CEO Douglas Conant, who sent more than 30,000 thank-you notes to his employees and customers over his ten years with the food company.[3] He didn't use text or email; each one was handwritten, celebrating the personal achievements of individuals. Did it make a difference? Yes, 100%. When Conant joined Campbell Soup in 2001, the business was failing badly. When he left, it was back on top and a regular winner of Gallup's Great Workplace award.

A little thanks goes a long way

STUDY: A little thanks goes a long way: explaining why gratitude expressions motivate prosocial behaviour[4]

A simple thank you can not only improve the feeling of self-worth in the person who receives the recognition, but it can also help them be better at their job. Researchers Adam Grant and Francesca Gino found that when we are made to feel we are capable and competent, we become more inclined to invest time and energy into our efforts because we believe it can lead to success.

For this experiment, the researchers focused on fundraisers seeking donations for a university, traditionally a thankless task which triggers rude feedback and frequent rejections. Those individuals who were thanked on a daily basis and told that their work was appreciated made 50% more calls to help the university and persisted longer without being asked than those who received little to no recognition.

Interestingly, Adam Grant, the Wharton Management professor who conducted the above research, also did a study with call-centre workers, which found gratitude is motivational and improves our mood.[5] For this study, half of the workers were asked to keep gratitude journals and write about things they appreciated. The other group was asked to keep journals and record things they had done that other people were grateful for. This second group was found to work harder and made more calls over the next few weeks compared to the employees who were focused on their own feelings of gratitude. By saying, 'I made a difference today and have something to offer', they felt better about themselves and performed better too.

Another study found that by increasing the amount of praise given to workers, organisations can realise a 24% improvement in the quality of their work, a 27% reduction in absenteeism and a 10% reduction in shrinkage or theft.[6] Similar findings came out of a survey with low-cost airline JetBlue, which scores highly in customer satisfaction and puts much of its success down to its internal programme of social recognition.[7] JetBlue found a 3% increase in retention and a 2% increase in engagement for every 10% increase in recognition. This translates into better performance with the data showing that engaged team members were *three times* more likely than disengaged members to woo their customers.

Showing gratitude is not just about how we make other people feel. When we show them appreciation or recognition, it has a positive impact on our own mental outlook too. When companies adopt a culture of praise and appreciation, it has a knock-on effect where teams become trusting with one other and likely to help each other as well. In other words, it plays a key role in creating the caring element that we talked about earlier. It also leads to increased happiness, satisfaction and resilience.

When we show our appreciation, it helps others with their confidence and self-esteem. Something else that often emerges in my sessions with clients is that a lot of them suffer from imposter syndrome, even if they hold senior positions. They don't feel they are good enough and this under-confidence is always there, nibbling away at their self-esteem.

When I dig into the reasons behind this (usually completely unfounded) insecurity, I invariably find that instances of praise and recognition are low in their companies. This is where small acts of appreciation can really play a part because they have a positive impact on confidence and self-esteem. As we know, individuals do pay it forward, so when people feel more confident about their roles, it has a positive impact on everybody else.

STUDY: The role of positivity and connectivity in the performance of business teams[8]

Carrot or stick? Praise or criticism? Which one is more effective when it comes to improving team performance?

This study found that both praise and criticism has its place, but what is most important is getting the ratio between them right. Researchers compared the response to positive comments, such as 'I agree with that' or 'That's a terrific idea', with that to negative comments like 'I don't agree with you' or 'We shouldn't even consider doing that'. When it comes to high-performing teams, the sweet spot is a ratio of 5.6:1, or nearly six positive comments for every negative one. Teams with medium performance showed a ratio of 1.9:1, or almost twice the number of positive to negative. When it came to low-performing teams, the ratio was 0.36:1, where team members were reporting almost three negative comments to each positive one.

There is, say the researchers, a need for some negative feedback, because it helps people overcome serious weaknesses, but when it is overdone, it can have a very detrimental impact on performance.

As outlined above, the tough messages do occasionally need to be delivered. The best advice is to do this regularly rather than once a year during a performance appraisal when it will have a negative impact. However, any criticism must be balanced out by praise in a ratio of above 5:1.

Motivation: Words are as good as cash

We all need to feel motivated at work. As the figures in the previous section show, it's key to productivity. There are, however, two different types of motivating factors: intrinsic and extrinsic.

Intrinsic motivation comes from within. It's where we do something because we enjoy it. We may keep our desk tidy because we like being organised or make a colleague coffee because we enjoy helping others. Extrinsic motivation, on the other hand, comes from outside factors. It's the motivation to accomplish a goal because of what we earn from it, such as a reward. Here, we keep our desk tidy because it is strict company policy or make a colleague coffee because we need their help on a difficult project.

Both motivating factors have their place, but it is in extrinsic motivation that leaders can play a crucial role. They can provide the rewards that encourage their teams into action, but here is the thing: while pay and perks are key extrinsic motivators, recognition and praise are just as effective.

STUDY: Processing of social and monetary rewards in the human striatum[9]

If you want to get something done, cash reigns supreme as an incentive, right? While increased pay and cash bonuses may be alluring for recruitment purposes and will boost performance, non-cash incentives such as a simple act of recognition or appreciation can be just as effective.

In this experiment, researchers used magnetic resource imaging to compare the impact of monetary versus social rewards on the brains of nineteen subjects. When the subjects felt their reputation enhanced by praise, it robustly activated the reward-related brain areas, most notably the striatum, the brain's reward hub. The brain processes verbal appreciation in the same way as a cash reward. They are a 'common neural currency', enhancing motivation in individuals.

We as leaders do also need to create an environment where people's intrinsic needs are met as well as their extrinsic needs, since both are crucial motivational forces and we need to achieve the right balance. To do this, we must recognise each person as an individual and play to their strengths. This means as far as possible allocating tasks according to those strengths and what makes team members feel intrinsically happy.

One of the simplest ways to motivate others extrinsically is to pay them a compliment. It is easy to do and costs nothing. Yet, as the study below shows, many of us underestimate the power of praise.

STUDY: Why a simple act of kindness is not as simple as it seems. Underestimating the positive impact of our compliments on others[10]

Do you feel awkward giving someone a compliment? A lot of people do, worrying it might seem insincere or be misinterpreted, or the person being given the compliment won't enjoy it. What many people don't realise is compliments have a much greater positive impact than they can ever have imagined.

In this study, people were asked to go out on to a college campus and give a compliment to someone of the same gender. Before they left to do this task, they were asked how they felt about giving compliments.

Once they had completed the task, the people who'd received the compliments, such as 'I like your shirt', were asked how they felt about the unexpected praise. In all cases, the compliment givers underestimated how what they said would make the other person feel. The individuals who received the compliments were happier, more pleased and flattered than the compliment giver had predicted.

Many of us are, at least partly, responsible for the widespread reluctance to give compliments. I know that whenever I'm given a compliment, I am often quick to dismiss it.

Someone might say, 'I like the way you delivered that talk; it was really informative.'

Before I know it, I'll shoot back, 'Oh no, I didn't do it as well as I had hoped. I think I stumbled a little in the first half. . .'

I am sure it must make the compliment giver reluctant to show any enthusiasm next time. Now I am aware of this, I have made much more effort to receive compliments gracefully. I thank the people who give me compliments because I know that will help them feel better too.

If you find yourself feeling awkward about giving compliments, the easiest way to get over it is to make the process more natural by doing it regularly. If an individual only says something nice about their co-worker once in a blue moon, then it's bound to feel a bit weird for both sides.

Recognition and appreciation need to be regular features of the working day. The frequency of positive reinforcement is more important than the intensity of it. The energy and glow we feel after we receive praise won't last forever, so before it disappears, it needs regular topping up.[11]

How to give effective recognition

In recent years, business leaders have realised the benefit of employee recognition programmes and 75% of organisations run one.[12] Yet not all initiatives are hitting the mark, a fact borne out by employee engagement scores which remain stubbornly static.

This could well be to do with the way these programmes are run. With recognition programmes, for example, employees will get a certificate for achieving a certain goal or be invited to a ceremony to celebrate a certain amount of years with their firm. Some people find this process a little bit formulaic and not very spontaneous. Plus, as I highlighted at the beginning of the chapter, waiting for a milestone can lead to vast gaps between acts of recognition. People don't retire on a daily basis or regularly celebrate milestones such as five or ten years of service.

There is another serious flaw with these types of initiatives, which is that they often overlook most of the team. It is only possible for one person to be 'salesperson of the month', even though the rest of the team may have been working their socks off.

A perhaps more effective tool is peer-to-peer recognition schemes, which are used in 41% of organisations.[13] The idea here is to encourage support and praise between co-workers so they acknowledge each other's skills and efforts towards particular goals. We all spend a great deal of time with our co-workers and to know that they appreciate and respect us can make a huge difference to our motivation levels.

Team leaders may need to formalise the process at first by setting aside time where employees are encouraged to voice what they appreciate about their peers or how much they contributed to a project. They could regularly do this at the beginning or end of meetings. It is an endeavour worth pursuing since peer-to-peer recognition programmes are 35.7% more effective than manager-only recognitions.[14]

Technology has made peer-to-peer recognition easier than ever before. There is a range of apps, including Nectar HR, Blueboard, Assembly, Kazoo HR and Kudos, which allow employees to log feedback on co-workers. They can run leader boards showing 'most supportive manager' or 'best department', which everyone can see.

Employees can nominate one another with peer-to-peer bonuses or points for going above and beyond or excelling at certain tasks. Over time, these points accumulate in a similar way to supermarket loyalty schemes. Everyone can see how everyone else is doing, which encourages an openness about discussing performance and further participation in the peer-to-peer recognition scheme. The apps tap into our human need to feel engaged and to recognise and reward the efforts of those around us.

When team leaders give recognition to their co-workers outside of these app-based systems, the compliment needs to be specific. Just telling someone 'Good job' or 'Great work' doesn't go far enough and can even come off as a little shallow and insincere. Instead, they should pick out some specifics.

'That was a powerful presentation yesterday,' they could say. 'You were to the point and I really appreciated those tips on how to concentrate more effectively. That will help me in the future.' Spelling out exactly what you got out of a piece of work or event immediately makes the compliment feel more authentic because it shows what an impact it had.

Another key part of being authentic with acts of recognition is for the person giving the praise to be clear in their own mind about *why* they are doing it. Most people will see through praise which is being given because a person feels sorry for them or wants to cheer them up. Only give recognition if there is a genuine reason for it. A good way to test this in your mind is to ask whether the action you're considering praising has had a real impact on you.

When you're celebrating a co-worker's achievements, it is crucial to do it as close as possible to the event or result that triggered the praise. If you leave it for weeks or even months after the event, the recognition becomes irrelevant.

Consider the delivery of the message. Not everyone on the team is the same. The extroverts will adore receiving recognition in a public way, but for introverts, this can be their worst nightmare. A private thank you will be much more appropriate. This is another reason why you as team leader need to know all the personality types on your team.

As Gary Chapman writes in his book *The 5 Languages of Appreciation in the Workplace*,[15] showing appreciation doesn't always need to be via words of praise, either publicly or in a private thank-you note. Managers can also show they value their team members by spending time with them, checking in to see how things are going. Take care not to ruin the impact of this by multitasking or answering emails while chatting; this is an instance where active listening can come into its own.

Another way of offering recognition and appreciation is through acts of service. This is where a co-worker recognises that another person in the team is working hard and offers to step in and help.

Finally, team leaders should always think carefully about everyone's role in an achievement. In any company, there are the star performers who bring home the big projects and regularly receive all the plaudits, but there are often countless people who have been involved every step of the way, working long hours and giving it their all. Don't let them become the unsung heroes. Their role may have been less visible, but it has been key and should receive equal appreciation.

Recognition and appreciation are key elements in a culture of caring and belonging. When we feel valued, we feel safe and that we are a part of something. In a culture where everyone regularly gives and receives praise, caring is self-perpetuating because the giver as well as the receiver will always feel good.

Summary

We all crave recognition and appreciation. When leaders say thank you often, a good feeling will permeate an organisation, creating trust and a lasting connection. It takes seconds to say and doesn't cost anything, yet it doesn't happen nearly enough.

In a business setting, it's to everyone's advantage to create a culture of recognition and appreciation. When people feel their efforts have been noticed, it encourages positivity, which in turn enhances the overall positive culture in the workplace. This has an impact on engagement and performance.

Afterword

The rise in remote and hybrid working arrangements has put employee wellbeing firmly in the spotlight. While the swing towards the 'new way of working' was fuelled by the pandemic, the truth is that the working environment had been shifting this way for some years beforehand. Technology has transformed the workplace, creating a culture where we feel like we are always on call, often buckling under the weight of an entirely unreasonable workload with little social support.

Organisation leaders around the world have known for some time that they need to properly consider what they are doing to engage their teams and balance the increasing demands of the always-on culture. Time is of the essence too. Rates of burnout, an occupational phenomenon defined as a chronic imbalance between job demands and job resources, are rising at an alarming rate.[16] Burnout is correlated with a range of mental and physical health challenges. Far too many employees are succumbing to symptoms such as extreme tiredness, reduced ability to regulate cognitive and emotional processes, anxiety and mental distance.

To be fair to many business leaders, they have responded. Initiatives abound, whether it is offering coaching or wellbeing days or yoga and meditation retreats. Around nine in ten companies have some sort of programme offering at least one kind of wellness benefit.[17] There has even been a little bit of competitiveness emerging in the shopping list of benefits on offer. Some businesses now include unlimited holidays in their benefits package to tempt people to join or stay longer.

However, these initiatives are not hitting the mark. As well as burnout rates continuing to rise, there is a range of other concerning indicators. As outlined in this book, we are firmly in the era of the Great Resignation. Record numbers of workers are quitting their jobs and looking for new, more personally fulfilling positions. They are getting out of workplaces they find toxic to protect themselves from burnout.

While I was writing this book, another phenomenon emerged: quiet quitting. This is where employees reject the idea that work is at the centre of their lives and that they must constantly go above and beyond to prove themselves. Instead, they take a deliberate step back from being fully invested in their roles, turning down challenging projects and refusing to answer work messages outside working hours.

If offering gyms, limitless holidays and wellness programmes is not going to reverse this trend, what is? How do employers stop their teams leaving or checking out of their jobs by doing just enough to get by?

The answer lies in changing the way we work. We need to properly address the issue of emotions and treat everyone as human beings. When they go to work, people want to feel emotionally engaged and connected. They seek a flexible, personalised human experience and strong relationships with their colleagues and team leaders.

While the pandemic accelerated the move towards hybrid working, it also showed us how to work together more effectively. During this intense period, there was a widespread recognition that many people were finding the sudden change in circumstance difficult. It forced employers to focus on the boundaries between the private and work lives in their teams.

As a result, employers devoted more time to regarding team members as people. Perhaps for the first time ever, many business leaders properly tackled the issue of emotions and realised that their staff are human beings who need to exchange feelings. Since this time, however, many companies have drifted back to business as usual.

This is a mistake. We need to continue the work which began during the pandemic. This means creating and maintaining proper emotional connections to build a network of people who feel secure and positive about their workplace.

People on the whole are social creatures with a fundamental need for emotional connection. Team leaders are perfectly positioned to facilitate this (although individuals can also benefit from understanding more about the pluses of emotionally positive cultures). There are many tips in this book on how to encourage an open dialogue among the team, which in turn creates a space for emotions and an opportunity for leaders to get to know their people and see them as whole humans rather than simply workers.

This will involve us as leaders taking the time to appreciate all our colleagues, to recognise what they do and to see them as the diverse and unique people they are. We need to make efforts to work on building communities among teams, even if they are working remotely. All of this needs to be backed by an endeavour to continually monitor emotions among individuals on the team.

As I have shown here in this book, emotions offer us valuable information. If we learn to read them, we will better understand what is going on inside individual members of the team. Initially, this process might not come easily to many. It may even involve investing a little more time than most team leaders feel they have to spare, but the payoff will be huge. It will have a massive impact on productivity and performance.

Forget about escalating perks and benefits. Forget about unlimited holidays. Instead, focus on helping people to find their sense of purpose so that they feel connected, part of a community, cared for and valued. This is the way to reduce burnout and see off quiet quitting.

Employers who do this won't simply be reshaping the workplace to bring it more in line with how people want to work today and to prepare us for a better future. They will be playing a pivotal role in helping people achieve significant improvements in their mental and physical wellbeing. That's a meaningful endeavour for everyone to get behind.

References

Chapter 1

1   Fuller, J; Kerr, W 'The Great Resignation didn't start with
    the pandemic' (*Harvard Business Review*, 2022) https://hbr.
    org/2022/03/the-great-resignation-didnt-start-with-the-
    pandemic, accessed 14 February 2023
2   Parker K; Horowitz JM 'Majority of workers who quit a
    job in 2021 cite low pay, no opportunities for advancement,
    feeling disrespected' (Pew Research Center, 2022) www.
    pewresearch.org/fact-tank/2022/03/09/majority-
    of-workers-who-quit-a-job-in-2021-cite-low-pay-no-
    opportunities-for-advancement-feeling-disrespected ,
    accessed 14 February 2023
3   'A call for accountability and action', *The Deloitte Global
    2021 Millennial and Gen Z Survey* (Deloitte, 2021) www.
    deloitte.com/content/dam/assets-shared/legacy/docs/
    insights/2022/2021-deloitte-global-millennial-survey-
    report.pdf, accessed 14 February 2023
4   Murray-Nevill, J '1 in 3 UK workers hide their true
    emotions at work' (Totaljobs, 2020) www.totaljobs.com/
    media-centre/1-in-3-uk-workers-hide-their-true-emotions-
    at-work, accessed 14 February 2023
5   Ibid

6   *2021 Mental Health at Work Report* (Mind Share
    Partners, 2021) www.mindsharepartners.org/
    mentalhealthatworkreport-2021
7   Walsh, C 'Young adults hardest hit by loneliness during
    pandemic' (*The Harvard Gazette*, 2021) https://news.
    harvard.edu/gazette/story/2021/02/young-adults-
    teens-loneliness-mental-health-coronavirus-covid-
    pandemic, accessed 14 February 2023
8   Masnick, G 'The rise of the single-person household' (Joint
    Center for Housing Studies of Harvard University, 2015)
    www.jchs.harvard.edu/blog/the-rise-of-the-single-person-
    household, accessed 14 February 2023
9   Harter, J 'U.S. employee engagement drops for first year
    in a decade' (Gallup Workplace, 2022) www.gallup.com/
    workplace/388481/employee-engagement-drops-first-
    year-decade.aspx, accessed 14 February 2023
10 Mackay, J 'Communication overload: Our research shows
    most workers can't go 6 minutes without checking email
    or IM' (RescueTime, 2018) https://blog.rescuetime.
    com/communication-multitasking-switches, accessed
    14 February 2023

Chapter 2

1   Poster, C 'The affections of the soul: Pathos, protreptic,
    and preaching in Hellenistic thought' in *Paul and Pathos*
    by Olbricht, T (Society of Biblical Literature, 2001) www.
    academia.edu/6135799/The_Affections_of_the_Soul_
    Pathos_Protreptic_and_Preaching_in_Hellenistic_Thought,
    accessed 30 January 2023
2   Schmitter, AM 'Ancient, Medieval and Renaissance
    theories of the emotions', *Stanford Encyclopedia of Philosophy*
    (Stanford University, 2021) https://plato.stanford.edu/
    entries/emotions-17th18th/LD1Background.html, accessed
    30 January 2023
3   Darwin, C *The Expression of the Emotions in Man and Animals*
    (John Murray, 1872)
4   Cannon, WB 'The James-Lange theory of emotions: A critical
    examination and an alternative theory', *The American*

Journal of Psychology, 39(1/4) (1927), 106-124, https://doi.
org/10.2307/1415404, accessed 15 February 2023

5   Schachter, S; Singer, J 'Cognitive, social, and physiological
determinants of emotional state', *Psychological Review*,
69/5 (1962), 379–399, https://doi.org/10.1037/h0046234,
accessed 30 January 2023

6   Lazarus, RS *Psychological Stress and the Coping Process*
(McGraw Hill, 1966)

7   Bolte Taylor, J *My Stroke of Insight* (Yellow Kite, 2009)

8   Ekman, P 'Basic Emotions' in *Handbook of Cognition and
Emotion* (John Wiley & Sons, 1999) www.paulekman.
com/wp-content/uploads/2013/07/Basic-Emotions.pdf,
accessed 2 February 2023

9   PERMA theory of well-being and PERMA workshops
(Penn Arts & Services, 2022) https://ppc.sas.upenn.
edu/learn-more/perma-theory-well-being-and-perma-
workshops, accessed 15 February 2023

10 Fredrickson, BL 'Positive emotions broaden and build',
Advances in Experimental Social Psychology, 47 (2013)
https://doi.org/10.1016/B978-0-12-407236-7.00001-2,
accessed 30 January 2023

11 Redwine, L; Henry, B; Pung, M; Wilson, K; Chinh, K;
Knight, B; Jain, S; Rutledge, T; Greenberg, B; Maisel, A;
Mills, P 'A pilot randomized study of a gratitude journaling
intervention on HRV and inflammatory biomarkers
in Stage B heart failure patients' (National Library of
Medicine, 2017) www.ncbi.nlm.nih.gov/pmc/articles/
PMC4927423, accessed 15 February 2023

12 Cregg, D; Cheavens, J 'Gratitude interventions: Effective
self-help? A meta-analysis of the impact on symptoms
of depression and anxiety' (Palgrave Macmillan, 2020)
https://link.springer.com/article/10.1007/s10902-020-
00236-6, accessed 15 February 2023

13 Ford, H 'How laughter benefits your heart health' (Henry
Ford Health, 2019) www.henryford.com/blog/2019/03/how-
laughter-benefits-heart-health, accessed 15 February 2023

14 Immordino-Yang, MH; Damasio, A 'We feel, therefore
we learn: The relevance of affective and social
neuroscience to education' (Wiley Online Library, 2007)
https://onlinelibrary.wiley.com/doi/10.1111/j.1751-
228X.2007.00004.x, accessed 15 February 2023

15 Hart, J 'Why creativity is the number one skill for
business success' (Blog post, Dale Carnegie, 2021)

www.dalecarnegie.com/blog/creativity-is-the-skill-for-business-success July 16, 2021, accessed 15 February 2023

16   Eastwood, J et al. 'The unengaged mind: Defining boredom in terms of attention', *Perspectives on Psychological Science*, 7 (2012) https://doi.org/10.1177/1745691612456044, accessed 30 January 2023

17   Forgas, J 'The upside of feeling down' (Sydney Symposium of Social Psychology, 2011) www.sydneysymposium.unsw.edu.au/2011/chapters/ForgasSSSP2011.pdf, accessed 15 February 2023

18   Brackett, M; Floman, J; Ashton-James, C; Cherkasskiy, L; Salovey, P 'The influence of teacher emotion on grading practices: A preliminary look at the evaluation of student writing' *Teachers and Teaching* 19/6 (2013), 634-646, https://doi.org/10.1080/13540602.2013.827453

19   Kahneman, D *Thinking, Fast and Slow* (Penguin, 2012)

20   Harter J, 'U.S. Employee engagement drops for first year in a decade' (Gallup Workplace, 2022) www.gallup.com/workplace/388481/employee-engagement-drops-first-year-decade.aspx

21   Maslow, AH 'A theory of human motivation' *Psychological Review*, 50/4 (1943) 370–396

22   Zenger, J; Folkman, J; Edinger, S *The Inspiring Leader: Unlocking the secrets of how extraordinary leaders motivate* (McGraw Hill, 2009)

23   Kingson, J 'Even your boss wants to quit' (Axios, 2022) www.axios.com/2022/06/22/ceo-csuite-burnout-pandemic-great-resignation, accessed 14 February 2023

24   *State of the global workplace: 2022 Report* (Gallup Workplace, 2022) www.gallup.com/workplace/349484/state-of-the-global-workplace-2022-report.aspx, accessed 14 February 2023

25   Witters, D 'Showing that you care about employee wellbeing' (Gallup Workplace, 2022) www.gallup.com/workplace/391739/showing-care-employee-wellbeing.aspx, accessed 14 February 2023

26   Girotti, M et al. 'Prefrontal cortex executive processes affected by stress in health and disease' (*Progress in Neuro-Psychopharmacology and Biological Psychiatry*, 13 July 2018) https://doi.org/10.1016/j.pnpbp.2017.07.004, accessed 2 February 2023

27   Luethi, M; Meier, B; Sandi, C 'Stress effects on working memory, explicit memory, and implicit memory for neutral

and emotional stimuli in healthy men' (*Frontiers in Behavioural Neuroscience, 30 November 2008*) www.ncbi.nlm.nih.gov/pmc/articles/PMC2628592, accessed 2 February 2023

28 Echouffo-Tcheugui, J; Conner, S; Himali, J; Maillard, P; DeCarli, C; Beiser, A; Vasan, R; Seshadri, S 'Circulating cortisol and cognitive and structural brain measures: The Framingham Heart Study' (National Library of Medicine, 2018) https://pubmed.ncbi.nlm.nih.gov/30355700, accessed 15 February 2023

29 Brooks et al.'The psychological impact of quarantine and how to reduce it: Rapid review of the evidence' (The Lancet, 2020) https://doi.org/10.1016/S0140-6736(20)30460-8, accessed 16 February 2023

Chapter 3

1 Katz, M 'Strategies for Managing Emotions: The process model of emotion regulation' *Attention Magazine* (December 2016) https://chadd.org/attention-article/strategies-for-managing-emotions-the-process-model-of-emotion-regulation, accessed 14 February 2023

2 Mischel, W; Shoda, Y; Rodriguez, ML 'Delay of gratification in children', *Science*, 244 (26 May 1989), www.science.org/doi/10.1126/science.2658056, accessed 30 January 2023

3 Goleman, D; Boyatzis, RE; McKee, *A Primal Leadership: Realizing the power of emotional intelligence* (Harvard Business School Press, 2002)

4 'Building the case for mindfulness in the workplace' (The Mindfulness Initiative, 2016) www.themindfulnessinitiative.org/Handlers/Download.ashx?IDMF=46ef10fd-4d64-41f9-91a6-163d52cd304c, accessed 15 February 2023

5 Goleman, D; Davidson, RJ *Altered Traits: Science reveals how meditation changes your mind, brain, and body* (Avery, 2017)

6 Greiser, C; Martini, JP; Meissner, N 'Unleashing the power of mindfulness in corporations' (BCG, 2018) www.bcg.com/publications/2018/unleashing-power-of-mindfulness-in-corporations, accessed 15 February 2023

7   'The ROI of a mindfulness program' (HEADSPACE) https://cdn2.hubspot.net/hubfs/4137181/hs_b2b_roi_ mindfulness_v4.pdf, accessed15 February 2023

8   Kircanski, K; Lieberman, MD; Craske, MG (2012) 'Feelings into words: Contributions of language to exposure therapy' *Psychological Science* 23/10 (2012), 1086-91. https://doi. org/10.1177/0956797612443830, accessed 20 February 2023

9   MasterClass Staff 'Jon Kabat-Zin's 6 tips for managing stress', MasterClass (7 June 2021), www.masterclass.com/ articles/stress-management-tips-from-jon-kabat-zinn, accessed 30 January 2023

Chapter 5

1   Zenger, J; Folkman, J 'What management style creates the highest level of employee satisfaction?' https:// zengerfolkman.com/leadership-studies, accessed 15 February 2023

2   'Power up: UK skills boosting transferable skills to achieve inclusive growth and mobility' (Deloitte, 2018) www2. deloitte.com/content/dam/Deloitte/uk/Documents/ Innovation/deloitte-uk-power-up-uk-skills.pdf, accessed 15 February 2023

3   Churchill F, 'Half of workers would consider changing roles if hybrid working was withdrawn, poll finds' (People Management, 2021) www.peoplemanagement. co.uk/article/1747324/half-workers-consider-changing- roles-hybrid-working-withdrawn-poll-finds, accessed 15 February 2023

4   Scott, BA; Colquitt, JA; Paddock, EL; Judge, TA 'A daily investigation of the role of manager empathy on employee well-being', Singapore Management University (2010), https://ink.library.smu.edu.sg/lkcsb_research/2965, accessed 30 January 2023

5   Cavallo, K; Brienza, D 'Emotional competence and leadership excellence at Johnson & Johnson' www. eiconsortium.org/reports/jj_ei_study.html, accessed 15 February 2023

6   For more reading about how to improve relationships like this, I recommend Scott, K *Radical Candor: How to get what you want by saying what you mean* (Pan, 2019)

7   Barsade, SG 'The ripple effect: Emotional contagion and its influence on group behaviour' (SAGE ASQ, 2002) https://web.media.mit.edu/~tod/media/pdfs/EmotionalContagion.pdf, accessed 15 February 2023

8   For further reading on this, I recommend: Brown, B *The Gifts of Imperfection* (Hazelden, 2018)

9   Moore, T 'The fight to save Tylenol (Fortune 1982) *Fortune* (7 October 2012) https://fortune.com/2012/10/07/the-fight-to-save-tylenol-fortune-1982, accessed 30 January 2023

10   Mehrabian, A; Ferris, SR 'Inference of attitudes from nonverbal communication in two channels' (*Journal of Consulting and Clinical Psychology*, 1967) https://doi.org/10.1037/h0024648, accessed 2 February 2023

11   Christian A 'Why hybrid work is emotionally exhausting' (BBC, 2022) www.bbc.com/worklife/article/20220120-why-hybrid-work-is-emotionally-exhausting, accessed 15 February 2023

12   Herway, J 'How to create a culture of psychological safety' (Gallup Workplace, 2017) www.gallup.com/workplace/236198/create-culture-psychological-safety.aspx, accessed 15 February 2023

Chapter 6

1   Taylor JM 'Mirror Neurons After a Quarter Century: New light, new cracks' Blog (SITN, Harvard University, 25 July 2016) https://sitn.hms.harvard.edu/flash/2016/mirror-neurons-quarter-century-new-light-new-cracks, accessed 15 February 2023

2   Parmar, B 'The most (and least) empathetic companies' (*Harvard Business Review*, 2015) https://hbr.org/2015/11/2015-empathy-index, accessed 15 February 2023

3   Van Bommel, T 'Empathic leaders drive employee engagement and innovation (Media release, Catalyst, 2021) www.catalyst.org/media-release/empathic-leaders-drive-

employee-engagement-and-innovation-media-release, accessed 15 February 2023

4   'Millenials or Gen Z: who's doing the most job-hopping' (CareerBuilder, no date) www.careerbuilder.com/advice/blog/how-long-should-you-stay-in-a-job, accessed 2 February 2023

5   Cuncic, A 'Why Gen Z is more open to talking about their mental health' (Verywell Mind, 2021) www.verywellmind.com/why-gen-z-is-more-open-to-talking-about-their-mental-health-5104730, accessed 15 February 2023

6   Violante, A 'Big tech and the big empathy gap' (textio, 2021) https://textio.com/blog/big-tech-and-the-big-empathy-gap/61568056905, accessed 15 February 2023

7   Ibid

8   Williams, R 'Why we need more empathy in the workplace' (LinkedIn, 2021) www.linkedin.com/pulse/why-we-need-more-empathy-workplace-ray-williams, accessed 15 February 2023

9   Ibid

10 Hardesty, L 'Study finds gender and skin-type bias in commercial artificial-intelligence systems' (MIT News, 2018) https://news.mit.edu/2018/study-finds-gender-skin-type-bias-artificial-intelligence-systems-0212, accessed 15 February 2023

11 2022 State of Workplace Empathy (Businessolver, 2022) www.businessolver.com/resources/state-of-workplace-empathy, accessed 15 February 2023

12 SWNS Staff 'More than half of Americans fear their employer would think less of them if they requested time off for mental health' (SWNS Digital, 2021) https://swnsdigital.com/us/2021/04/more-than-half-of-americans-fear-their-employer-would-think-less-of-them-if-they-requested-time-off-for-mental-health, accessed 15 February 2023

13 2022 State of Workplace Empathy (Businessolver, 2022) www.businessolver.com/resources/state-of-workplace-empathy, accessed 15 February 2023

14 For more on this, I recommend: Hastings, R; Meyer, E *No Rules Rules: Netflix and the culture of reinvention* (Virgin Books, 2020)

Chapter 7

1   Solomon, L 'Two-thirds of managers are uncomfortable communicating with employees, (*Harvard Business Review*, 2016) https://hbr.org/2016/03/two-thirds-of-managers-are-uncomfortable-communicating-with-employees, accessed 15 February 2023
2   Bravely 'The cost of the conversation gap on workplace health' (Bravely, 2009) https://learn.workbravely.com/cost-of-the-conversation-gap, accessed 15 February 2023
3   McLain, D; Nelson, B 'How fast feedback fuels performance' (Gallup Workplace, 2022) www.gallup.com/workplace/357764/fast-feedback-fuels-performance.aspx, accessed 15 February 2023

Chapter 8

1   Heath, K; Flynn, J 'How women can show passion at work without seeming "emotional"' (Harvard Business Review, 2015) https://hbr.org/2015/09/how-women-can-show-passion-at-work-without-seeming-emotional, accessed 15 February 2023
2   Weigard, A; Loviska, AM; Beltz, AM 'Little evidence for sex or ovarian hormone influences on affective variability' (Scientific Reports, 2021) www.nature.com/articles/s41598-021-00143-7, accessed 15 February
3   McRae, K et al. 'Gender differences in emotion regulation: An fMRI study of cognitive reappraisal', *Group Processes & Intergroup Relations*, 11/2 (2008) https://doi.org/10.1177/1368430207088035, accessed 30 January 2023
4   Collier L, 'Why we cry' (APA, 2014) www.apa.org/monitor/2014/02/cry, accessed 15 February 2023
5   Murray-Nevill, J '1 in 3 workers hide their true emotions at work' (Totaljobs, 2020) www.totaljobs.com/media-centre/1-in-3-uk-workers-hide-their-true-emotions-at-work, accessed 15 February 2023
6   Accountemps, 'Cry me a river: How emotions are perceived in the workplace' (Cision, 2018) www.prnewswire.com/news-releases/cry-me-a-river-how-emotions-are-perceived-in-the-workplace-300623153.html, accessed 15 February 2023

7   Ibid

8   Brescoll, V; Uhlmann, EL 'Can an angry woman get ahead?:
    Status conferral, gender, and expression of emotion in
    the workplace' (*Psychological Science*, 2008) https://gap.
    hks.harvard.edu/can-angry-woman-get-ahead-status-
    conferral-gender-and-expression-emotion-workplace,
    accessed 15 February 2023

9   Barry, K 'Recruiting women takes more than just
    competitive pay' (Gallup Workplace, 2022) www.gallup.
    com/workplace/390275/recruiting-women-takes-more-
    than-competitive-pay.aspx, accessed 15 February 2023

10 Taylor, CL et al.'Gender and emotions at work:
    Organizational rank has greater emotional benefits for men
    than women', *Sex Roles* (2022) https://doi.org/10.1007/
    s11199-021-01256-z, accessed 30 January 2023

11 Sutherland, R 'Tackling the root causes of suicide' (Blog post,
    NHS 75 England, 2018) www.england.nhs.uk/blog/tackling-
    the-root-causes-of-suicide, accessed 15 February 2023

12 Brent, A; Kohanim, J; Tekle, F 'New survey from Citi
    and LinkedIn explores the factors that shape men's and
    women's professional paths – and their varied definitions
    of success', Business Wire (30 October 2013) www.
    businesswire.com/news/home/20131030005200/en/New-
    Survey-from-Citi-and-LinkedIn-Explores-the-Factors-that-
    Shape-Men's-and-Women's-Professional-Paths-—-and-Their-
    Varied-Definitions-of-Success, accessed 30 January 2023

13 Williams, J; Cuddy, A 'Will working mothers take your
    company to court?' (*Harvard Business Review*, 2012) https://
    hbr.org/2012/09/will-working-mothers-take-your-
    company-to-court, accessed 15 February 2023

14 Daily Briefing 'How often are women interrupted by men?
    Here's what the research says' (Advisory Board, 2017)
    www.advisory.com/daily-briefing/2017/07/07/men-
    interrupting-women, accessed 15 February 2023

Chapter 9

1   Brassey, J; Coe, E; Dewhurst, M; Enomoto, K; Giarola,
    R; Herbig, B; Jeffery, B 'Addressing employee burnout:

Are you solving the right problem?' (McKinsey Health Institute, 2022) www.mckinsey.com/mhi/our-insights/addressing-employee-burnout-are-you-solving-the-right-problem, accessed 15 February 2023

2 'Switzerland is the best place for a career abroad' (expatnetwork) www.expatnetwork.com/switzerland-is-best-place-for-a-career-abroad, accessed 15 February 2023

3 Charaba, C 'Employee retention: The real cost of losing an employee' (PeopleKeep, 28 June 2022) www.peoplekeep.com/blog/employee-retention-the-real-cost-of-losing-an-employee, accessed 31 January 2023

4 'Your business strategy hinges on employee engagement' (Gallup Workplace, 2023) www.gallup.com/workplace/229424/employee-engagement.aspx, accessed 15 February 2023

5 Morrison, C '16 employee burnout statistics you can't ignore' (EveryoneSocial, 2022) https://everyonesocial.com/blog/employee-burnout-statistics, accessed 15 February 2023

6 'Gallup Daily: U.S. employee engagement' (Gallup, no date) https://news.gallup.com/poll/180404/gallup-daily-employee-engagement.aspx, accessed 31 January 2023

7 Jouany, V; Mäkipää, M '8 employee engagement statistics you need to know in 2023' (Haiilo, 2022) https://haiilo.com/blog/employee-engagement-8-statistics-you-need-to-know, accessed 15 February 2023

8 'Gallup Daily: U.S. Employee Engagement' (Gallup, no date), https://news.gallup.com/poll/180404/gallup-daily-employee-engagement.aspx, accessed 17 February 2023

9 Kolb, D *Experimental Learning: Experience as the source of learning and development* (Prentice Hall, January 1984)

10 O'Neill, O; Rothbard, N 'Is love all you need? The effects of emotional culture, suppression and work-family conflict on firefighter risk-taking and health' *Academy of Management Journal*, 60 (14 December 2015) https://journals.aom.org/doi/abs/10.5465/amj.2014.0952, accessed 31 January 2023

11 O'Brien, G 'Sigal Barsade and getting culture right' (Business Ethics, 2022) https://business-ethics.com/2022/05/28/sigal-barsade-and-getting-culture-right, accessed 15 February 2023

Chapter 10

1   Allen, KA; Gray, D; Baumeister, R; Leary, M 'The need to belong: A deep dive into the origins, implications, and future of a foundational construct' (Springer Link, 2021) https://link.springer.com/article/10.1007/s10648-021-09633-6#ref-CR6, accessed 15 February 2023

2   Brown, B *The Power of Vulnerability: Teachings on authenticity, connection and courage* (Sounds True INC, 2013)

3   Brown, B 'The power of vulnerability' (2011) www.ted.com/talks/brene_brown_the_power_of_vulnerability?utm_campaign=tedspread&utm_medium=referral&utm_source=tedcomshare, accessed 31 January 2023

4   Eisenberger, N; Lieberman, M; Williams, K 'Does rejection hurt? An FMRI study of social exclusion' (National Library of Medicine, 2003) https://pubmed.ncbi.nlm.nih.gov/14551436, accessed 15 February 2023

5   Ekman, P 'Universals and cultural differences in facial expressions of emotion' (*Nebraska Symposium on Motivation*, 1971) https://psycnet.apa.org/record/1973-11154-001, accessed 31 January 2023

6   Ekman, P et al. 'Universals and cultural differences in the judgements of facial expressions of emotion' (1973) www.paulekman.com/wp-content/uploads/2013/07/Universals-And-Cultural-Differences-In-The-Judgment-Of-Facia.pdf, accessed 15 February 2023

7   Schwartz, J; Mallon, D; Denny, B; Van Durme, Y; Hauptmann, M; Yan, R; Poynton, S 'Belonging: From comfort to connection to contribution' (Deloitte, 2020) www2.deloitte.com/us/en/insights/focus/human-capital-trends/2020/creating-a-culture-of-belonging.html, accessed 15 February 2023

8   Mermelshtine, R 'Bringing your true self to work: Is there a price to covering your true personality?' (Totaljobs) www.totaljobs.com/advice/bringing-your-true-self-to-work-is-there-a-price-to-covering-your-personality, accessed 15 February 2023

9   Holt-Lunstad, J; Smith, T 'Loneliness and social isolation as risk factors for CVD: Implications for evidence-based patient care and scientific inquiry' (*BMJ*, 2016) https://heart.bmj.com/content/102/13/987, accessed 15 February 2023

10 'The loneliness epidemic persists: A post-pandemic look at the state of loneliness among U.S. adults' (Cigna News, 2021) https://newsroom.cigna.com/loneliness-epidemic-persists-post-pandemic-look, accessed 15 February 2023

11 Dixon-Fyle, S; Dolan, K; Hunt, V; Prince, S 'Diversity wins: How inclusion matters' (McKinsey & Company, 2020) www.mckinsey.com/featured-insights/diversity-and-inclusion/diversity-wins-how-inclusion-matters, accessed 15 February 2023

12 Waders, P 'The power of belonging' (YouTube, 2016) www.youtube.com/watch?v=xwadscBnlhU, accessed 31 January 2023

13 Smith, Dr C; Yoshino, K 'Uncovering talent: a new model of inclusion' (Deloitte, 2019) www2.deloitte.com/content/dam/Deloitte/us/Documents/about-deloitte/us-about-deloitte-uncovering-talent-a-new-model-of-inclusion.pdf, accessed 16 February 2023

14 Lindsey, A; King E; Hebl, M; Levine, N 'The impact of method, motivation, and empathy on diversity training effectiveness' (Springer Link, 2014) https://link.springer.com/article/10.1007/s10869-014-9384-3, accessed 15 February 2023

Chapter 11

1 Barsade, S; O'Neill, O 'What's love got to do with it?: The influence of a culture of companionate love in the long-term care setting' (*SAGE* Journals, 2014) https://journals.sagepub.com/doi/abs/10.1177/0001839214538636, accessed 15 February 2023

2 Hamilton, K; Sandhu, R; Hamill, L 'The Science of care' (Limeade Institute, 2019) www.limeade.com/wp-content/uploads/2019/09/LimeadeInstitute_TheScienceOfCare_Whitepaper_Web.pdf, accessed 15 February 2023

3 'Our Publications and Research' (Utopia) www.weareutopia.co/publications, accessed 15 February 2023

4 Maslow, AH 'A theory of human motivation' *Psychological Review*, 50/4 (1943), 370-396

5 Newsroom 'Gartner HR research shows organizations must re-invent their employee value proposition to deliver a

more human deal' (Gartner, 2021) www.gartner.com/en/
newsroom/press-releases/2020-05-25-gartner-hr-research-
shows-organizations-must-reinvent-their-employment-
value-proposition-to-deliver-a-more-human-deal, accessed
15 February 2023

6   Chancellor, J; Margolis, S; Jacobs Bao, K; Lyubomirsky,
    S 'Everyday prosociality in the workplace: The
    reinforcing benefits of giving, getting and glimpsing'
    (University of California, 2018) http://sonjalyubomirsky.
    com/files/2019/04/Chancellor-Margolis-Bao-
    Lyubomirsky-2018.pdf, accessed 15 February 2023

7   Joly, J 'Four-day week: Which countries have embraced
    it and how's it going so far?' (euronews.next, 2022)
    www.euronews.com/next/2022/06/06/the-four-day-week-
    which-countries-have-embraced-it-and-how-s-it-going-so-
    far, accessed 15 February 2023

Chapter 12

1   Parker, K; Horowitz, J 'Majority of workers who quit a job
    in 2021 cite low pay, no opportunities for advancement,
    feeling disrespected' (Pew Research Center, 2022) www.
    pewresearch.org/fact-tank/2022/03/09/majority-
    of-workers-who-quit-a-job-in-2021-cite-low-pay-no-
    opportunities-for-advancement-feeling-disrespected,
    accessed 15 February 2023

2   Cariaga, V 'Nearly half of Americans quit their jobs
    because they feel unappreciated by management' (Yahoo!
    Finance, 2022) https://finance.yahoo.com/news/
    nearly-half-americans-quit-jobs-145250545.html, accessed
    2 February 2023, accessed 15 February 2023

3   Reeves, J 'How thank-you notes saved a dying company'
    (Blog post, Lawyers Mutual, 2016) www.lawyersmutualnc.
    com/blog/how-thank-you-notes-saved-a-dying-company,
    accessed 15 February 2023

4   Grant, A; Gino, F 'A little thanks goes a long way:
    Explaining why gratitude expressions motivate prosocial
    behavior' *Journal of Personality and Social Psychology*,
    98/6 (2010), 946-955, www.umkc.edu/facultyombuds/

documents/grant_gino_jpsp_2010.pdf, accessed
15 February 2023

5   Grant, A et al. 'Impact and the art of motivation
maintenance: The effects of contact with beneficiaries on
persistence behavior' (*Organizational Behavior and Human
Decision Processes*, May 2007) https://doi.org/10.1016/j.
obhdp.2006.05.004, accessed 31 January 2023

6   *State of the American Workplace report* (Gallup Workplace)
www.gallup.com/workplace/238085/state-american-
workplace-report-2017.aspx, accessed 15 February 2023

7   Achor S, 'The benefits of Peer-to-Peer praise at work'
(*Harvard Business Review*, 2016) https://hbr.org/2016/02/
the-benefits-of-peer-to-peer-praise-at-work, accessed
15 February 2023

8   Losada, M; Heaphy, E 'The role of positivity and
connectivity in the performance of business teams:
A nonlinear dynamics model' (*SAGE* Journals, 2016)
https://journals.sagepub.com/doi/abs/10.1177/000276420
3260208?journalCode=absb, accessed 16 February 2023

9   Izuma K; Saito D; Sadato N, 'Processing of Social and
Monetary rewards in the Human Striatum' (*Science
Direct*, 2008) www.sciencedirect.com/science/article/pii/
S0896627308002663, accessed 15 February 2023

10 Boothby, EJ; Bohns, VK 'Why a simple act of kindness is
not as simple as it seems. Underestimating the positive
impact of our compliments on others' (*SAGE* Journals,
2020) https://doi.org/10.1177/0146167220949003, accessed
16 February 2023

11 Boothby, E; Zhao, X; Bohns, V 'A simple compliment can
make a big difference' (*Harvard Business Review*, 2021)
https://hbr.org/2021/02/a-simple-compliment-can-make-
a-big-difference, accessed 15 February 2023

12 Duffy, J '25 great statistics on employee recognition' (More
Than Accountants, 2020) www.morethanaccountants.
co.uk/25-great-statistics-employee-recognition, accessed
15 February 2023

13 Ibid

14 Ibid

15 Chapman, G *The 5 Languages of Appreciation in the Workplace:
Empowering organizations by encouraging people* (Moody, 2012)

16 'Addressing employee burnout: Are you solving the
right problem?' (McKinsey Health Institute, 2022) www.
mckinsey.com/mhi/our-insights/addressing-employee-

burnout-are-you-solving-the-right-problem , accessed 15 February 2023

17   Lieberman C, 'What wellness programs don't do for workers' (*Harvard Business Review*, 2019) https://hbr. org/2019/08/what-wellness-programs-dont-do-for-workers, accessed 15 February 2023

18   Rae, E *DAD: Untold stories of fatherhood, love, mental health & masculinity* (MusicFootballFatherhood, 2021)

19   Whitty-Collins, G *Why Men Win At Work:.. And how we can make inequality history* (Luath, 2021)

Acknowledgements

Many thanks to my husband, Fabrice, Dorine van der Wal and Niki Parker whose unwavering support and love made all the difference and motivated me to reach the finishing line. A special thank you to Penny Andrea and Miranda Quinney, my first readers, who gave me their honest and expert feedback.

A number of contributors have enriched the content of this book, complementing my own experience and research with highly relevant and interesting viewpoints of their own. I wish to take the opportunity here to thank every one of them and allow them to tell you a little about themselves.

Anne Sophie Eyméoud, Director General of Rothschild & Co Wealth Management, Belgium.
Mother of three children, Anne Sophie has been active in the financial world for over twenty years. She is managing director of the Belgian branch of

Rothschild & Co and a group partner with duties in environmental, social and governance, and philanthropic matters, as well as the balance and inclusion and new gen programmes.

Anne Sophie is passionate about leadership and impact. She has been substantially involved in philanthropy from an early age and enjoys building bridges between the business and the philanthropic worlds through thematic workshops in philanthropy and charitable activities in different foundations.

Christiane Bisanzio, Thought Leader, Diversity and Inclusion.
An internationally recognised HR executive and thought leader in diversity, equity and inclusion (DE&I), Christiane has been working in HR for more than twenty years and has held leadership positions in General Electric and AXA. Christiane was included three consecutive years in the Global Diversity List of Top 50 Leaders by *The Economist* for her work in DE&I.

Dr Rebecca Nicholson, Author of *The Conflict Doctor*, Researcher and Strategist.
A podcast host, consultant, trainer, researcher and author, Rebecca has worked with leaders across sectors and cultures. She specialises in conflict – at all the complex levels it originates, exists, and affects us – mental, emotional, spiritual and physical. Rebecca has over twenty years of experience working in complex roles that include conflict, strategic communication and behavioural intelligence

Her expertise is in the areas of violent and political conflict, purposeful leadership and impactful relationships. An expert-level critical thinker and agile communicator, Rebeca helps clients articulate multifaceted conflict issues clearly and succinctly, decode subtle points of negotiation and discover hidden possibilities for growth, learning and expansion. Her cross-functional field experience was developed in West Africa, South America, Far East, MENA and Europe, in initiatives that included military special forces, indigenous populations, private companies, NGOs, policy makers, media outlets and tribal leaders.

Elliott Rae, Founder and Editor-in-chief of Music. Football. Fatherhood.
This highly successful parenting platform has been called the 'Mumsnet for Dads' by the BBC. Elliott is the author of bestselling book *DAD*,[18] a deeply moving collection of twenty stories that represent the diversity of modern fatherhood and challenge the traditional ideas of masculinity. Elliott has been recognised by the United Nations for his work on gender equality and was awarded the #HeForShe award by UN Women UK. He has been featured in *The Independent* and *The Telegraph*, and appeared live on *Loose Women*, the BBC News, Channel 4 and Radio 5 Live.

Frederic Van Mullem, Vice President HR, Medtronic.
Frederic is an HR executive with a proven track record and diverse service and industry experience in all functional areas of HR management, including the chief

HR officer role. He is a performer in the international arena, adept at direct-line and cross-functional management within complex organisations. He also has deep international insight and multicultural expertise acquired while working and living in Europe, North America and Asia-Pacific.

With thirty years in progressively senior roles in legal and HR, Frederic has amassed significant experience across multiple industries ranging from pharmaceuticals, chemicals, industrial and infrastructure services, to high-tech capital equipment and, more recently, medical devices.

Gill Whitty-Collins, Writer and Gender Equality Warrior.

Gill is the author of *Why Men Win At Work:.. And how we can make inequality history.*[19] She was born near Liverpool in 1970, the youngest of three sisters, and after attending the local comprehensive school, she went on to study at Cambridge University. Upon graduating, she joined Procter & Gamble (P&G), where she led global brands such as Olay, Always and Pantene and swiftly moved up the ladder to marketing director, general manager and finally senior vice president. Gill now works as a keynote speaker, NED, consultant, trainer and executive coach.

Hajar El Haddaoui, Senior Director, Executive Board Member.

Alongside her 'side job' as an advisor/consultant, Hajar El Haddaoui is a senior director and member of the executive board at NTT Switzerland and has been in the IT industry for over eighteen years. She has held global and regional roles focused on corporate strategy, transformation, change and innovation. Her passion lies in creating inclusive and empathetic work environments in which people are encouraged and supported to be the best they can as their most authentic selves.

Hajar was granted the Business Leader Award for Best All-round Female in IT in Europe. She is a member of the advisory board of MOD-ELLE, of the advisory council of WINconference, a frequent public speaker and an active contributor to inclusive leadership and advocate for the Sustainable Development Goals.

John McCusker, Global Vice President of Talent Management, Bacardi.
After a childhood in Scotland, John moved to England, on to Spain, through the Middle East, across to Manhattan, down to Brazil, and then back to Europe. Picking up Spanish, Portuguese and French along the way has been only a part of an enriching journey that keeps evolving. To his people in Bacardi, he describes himself as a fitness coach, helping them to build the skills and capabilities to be ready to face the challenges of the future. John is passionate about building a world filled with goodness, gratitude and grit.

Michael A Piker, Global DE&I and Reward Director, Flutter Entertainment.
Mike has over thirty years of global HR executive experience working in total rewards, DE&I, talent

mobility and people analytics. His corporate experience includes working with Flutter Entertainment, Philip Morris International, Naspers/Prosus, Lenovo, Syngenta, Alcoa, Cisco and consulting experience with Mercer, Buck and ORC Worldwide. He has worked in nine countries including Japan, China, Singapore, Brazil and Switzerland, and currently lives in London where he works for Flutter Entertainment Plc. Mike has served on WorldatWork Global Advisory Council and has lectured at Erasmus, New York University.

Nienke Mulder, CHRO, The Global Fund.
Nienke Mulder is CHRO at The Global Fund in Geneva, Switzerland. She is passionate about global health and is excited to contribute with her team to The Global Fund's mission and to leverage the power of its people to successfully deliver its new strategy.

Nienke has extensive experience and more than two decades of leadership and expertise in HR, change management and diversity and inclusion. From January 2017 until February 2022, Nienke was based at GlaxoSmithKline, where she was a global change director, global inclusion and diversity strategy lead and the HR director for Switzerland.

She has a passion for volunteering and contributing to society and has participated in programmes to raise funds, build capability, mentor and develop business cases for non-government organisations and other public-private partnership initiatives. In addition, she regularly delivers guest lectures at universities.

Rubén Alejandro, Group Head Diversity and Inclusion, Syngenta Group.
Born in Mexico and living in Switzerland, Ruben is a proud member of the LGBTQI+ community and currently leads the DE&I strategy for the Syngenta Group and its 50,000 people across more than 100 countries. Passionate about DE&I, he guides and supports leaders to embed this as part of the business agenda and priorities. Ruben holds two master's degrees and has over fifteen years of experience in global corporations from various industries such as automotive, financial services and life science.

Sameer Chauhan, Director of UNICC.
Sameer joined the UNICC in 2015 and was appointed director by the UN Secretary-General António Guterres in December 2019. As director, he has the responsibility to lead all aspects of UNICC's strategy and operations. He has over twenty years of prior experience in both public and private sectors.

Sameer has a wife and two daughters with whom he enjoys exploring new places and discovering new cuisines.

Shazia Ginai, Chief Growth Officer, Catalyx.
Shazia leads the global growth strategy for Catalyx, a strategy and insight agency. She has a track record of successfully building and leading insight capability and embedding this into organisations to drive action across multiple markets and functions.

Prior to joining Catalyx, she worked across the luxury-fragrance and skin-care brands at P&G, led the global insight function at ghd and, most recently, was the CEO of Neuro-Insight in the UK. Shazia is one of the co-founders of the Women in Research Accelerate programme, board chair for Colour of Research and a member of the Market Research Society's Diversity and Inclusion Council. She has a passion for driving awareness and research into menstrual health, actively volunteering for Endometriosis UK.

Xiangchen Zhang, Deputy Director-General, WTO. Ambassador Xiangchen Zhang formerly held senior positions in the Chinese government, including vice minister of commerce and permanent representative of China to the WTO. He has had an extensive career of more than thirty years in international affairs and trade negotiations. Zhang holds a bachelor's degree in law, a master's degree in international relations and a PhD in international politics from Peking University.

The Author

Natalie is an author, executive coach, consultant and keynote speaker with over 30 years' experience in the corporate world working in senior management roles in the private sector and the UN. Today she is the CEO and Founder of HumanForce, an international consultancy working with organisations to build healthy and resilient cultures that drive performance. She is a highly experienced, commercial and versatile professional with a consistent track record of successful delivery of tangible results.

As a coach and consultant Natalie works closely with leaders and teams to unleash the potential and strength of their human capital. Her work is focused on developing emotionally intelligent leaders and teams and delivering programmes that foster belonging, engagement and care at all levels of an organisation. She has worked closely with multinationals from a variety of sectors including Pharma, FMCG, Sports and Luxury, and also various UN organisations. Natalie is an engaging TEDx speaker and has also delivered key-note speeches for companies, business schools and leadership programmes worldwide.

She grew up in Hertfordshire, England and for the past twenty-two years has been based in Geneva, Switzerland.

Find out more at:

🌐 www.human-force.ch

in www.linkedin.com/in/natalieboudouexecutive coach